Geonomic 3:

Advancen PUTTING FOOD ON WHAT WAS THE

Michael P. (SOVIET TABLE

Putting Food on What Was the Soviet Table

Edited by Michael P. Claudon
and Tamar L. Gutner

Geonomics Special Report and Policy Statement

NEW YORK UNIVERSITY PRESS
New York and London

Library of Congress Cataloging-in-Publication Data

Putting food on what was the Soviet table
/edited by Michael P. Claudon and Tamar L. Gutner
p. cm. (The Geonomics special report and policy statement series)

Papers presented at a Geonomics seminar, October 17-20, 1991
Includes bibliographical references.
ISBN 0-8147-1476-5 (cloth) — ISBN 0-8147-1477-3 (pbk.)
1. Food supply — Government policy — Soviet Union — Congresses.
2. Food industry and trade — Government policy — Soviet Union —
Congresses.
3. Produce trade— Government policy — Soviet Union — Congresses.
4. Agriculture and state — Soviet Union — Congresses.
5. Farm produce — Soviet Union— Marketing — Congresses.
6. Food prices — Soviet Union — Congresses.
7. Collectives farms — Soviet Union — Congresses.
8. Land Reform — Soviet Union—Congresses.
9. Food Relief — Soviet Union — Congresses.
I. Claudon, Michael P. II. Gutner, Tamar L. III. Series
HD9015.S652G48 1992
338.1 '947 — dc20

91-47646

CIP

Contents

Acknowledgments

The Geonomics Fall 1991 Seminar, October 17-20, "From Field to Table: Reforming Soviet Agriculture," was generously supported by the Institute's corporate sponsors: The Dun & Bradstreet Corporation; Heytesbury, Inc.; Holstein Association; Jones International, Inc.; Josephine Bay Paul & C. Michael Paul Foundation, Inc.; Scott-European Corporation; and Sharpoint.

Also supporting the seminar were Bread Loaf Construction Company, Inc.; Cargill, Inc.; Ebony Bull Capital Corporation; The International Bank Credit Analyst; Scott and Aida Pardee; Joseph E. Seagram & Sons, Inc.; Sheffield Group, Ltd; and Russian Interpreting Services, Inc.

Reforming Soviet agriculture will be a daunting task. Conceptualizing themes, organizing the seminar, and bringing together 40 busy people from points halfway around the world can seem equally daunting.

The Geonomics staff, for the most part, remained undaunted by schedules that changed almost daily, incompatible computer disks, and airlines that said you couldn't get here from there.

My special thanks to Nancy Ward, seminar coordinator, who once again proved that the impossible merely takes a little longer.

Tamar Gutner, the Institute's research director, was instrumental in assembling a diverse, engaging group of Soviet and Western agricultural experts with the help of Vikram Capoor, the Institute's research assistant. Tamar was also my right hand in helping prepare the papers for this book.

As in the past, we deeply appreciate the support of staff, faculty, and students of Middlebury College and the use of College facilities. There are few places more conducive to good conversation after a long day of meetings than the porch at the College's Bread Loaf Inn.

Finally, a special thanks to Vera Matusevich, who was responsible for bringing together an outstanding group of Russian and Estonian agricultural experts.

Michael P. Claudon
President
Geonomics Institute

Introduction

S oviet agriculture, despite years of heavy state investment and sub-
sidies, cannot feed its people.
• Soviet agriculture has performed well and overall production of
Soviet agriculture increased by 12 percent from 1985 to 1990.

• Soviet consumers, especially in the cities, must spend hours in lines,
often in vain, for fresh fruit, vegetables, and good meat.

• Soviet consumers have diets comparable to other industrialized
countries and only face shortages at relatively high levels of consumption.

• Soviet farmers produced more wheat, dairy products, vegetables, and
small grains, such as oats, barley, and rye, than the United States did in 1990.

• The production-conscious Soviet Union spends far less than the
United States on food processing and distribution. Twenty to 50 percent of
its harvests never reach the consumer.

These often seemingly contradictory statements illustrate both the
enormous problems and the potential of Soviet agriculture. Very simply, the
Soviet Union has the potential to feed its people well and to be an exporter
of food.

But Soviet agriculture also has a host of systemic problems: an inadequate infrastructure, from roads to warehouses; government-subsidized
prices that do not reflect the cost of production or the value of goods;
independence-minded republics and state enterprises that ignore orders
from the disintegrating central government; an apprehensive, urban population that hoards produce and exacerbates shortages; rising food prices
that break family budgets; and bureaucrats who block needed reforms.

The Geonomics Fall Gateway Seminar, "From Field to Table: Reforming Soviet Agriculture," brought together 40 Soviet and Western agricultural specialists from October 17-20, 1991, to assess the state of Soviet

agriculture and to develop recommendations to speed agricultural reform.

The 11 papers and presentations that follow do just that. They look broadly at the state of the Soviet economy and agricultural reforms and at the role of the West in spurring reform and creating markets for Western goods and technology. They also examine in greater detail specific reforms, such as land reform, the cooperative movement, and the development of private farms.

The first four papers present an overview of the Soviet economy, in general, and the agricultural economy, in particular. Business consultant John Cavanaugh in his seminar keynote address argues that the West can best aid the Soviet Union by providing long-term, technical assistance programs that help the Soviets develop a coherent market economy. The American food industry can provide the management advice and technology to raise the quality and quantity of Soviet food production to world standards. The U.S. government, in turn, must move beyond its single-minded emphasis on promoting grain trade and develop a comprehensive policy that promotes all our economic interests.

Sovietologist Keith Bush examines the rapid decline of the Soviet economy: near hyperinflation, a 15 to 20 percent drop in the GNP, a budget deficit of nearly 20 percent of GNP. Despite a raft of reform proposals in the past two years, the country still has no "coherent economic plan." The new union treaty is a "declaration of intent...(not) a viable and binding detailed agreement" and does not confront critical issues such as price decontrol and privatization. But the "good news" is that the Soviet Union remains a wealthy country in resources and in its educated people; there is an increase in entrepreneurial and free-market activities; and the post-Cold War West has jointly resolved to help during this critical transition period.

Distribution, Not Harvest Size, Is Main Problem

Soviet agricultural economist Vladimir Tikhonov, in assessing this year's "food crisis," argues that the shortages are caused by an extremely inefficient food distribution system, not a poor harvest. State farms, upset with low government prices, are no longer meeting government orders and are compounding "shortages" in state stores. To correct the crisis, the government must immediately legalize and stimulate free trade in all spheres and transform state and collective farms into a system of free and marketable peasant farms.

In addition to the system's widespread distribution problems, German economist Karl-Eugen Wädekin cites the government's inflationary monetary policy as a major cause of the food crisis. Incomes are rising far faster than food output, and regional inequalities are increasing. Like Mr. Cavanaugh, he argues that the West can best promote reform through training programs for private farmers and food administrators. Food aid, he argues, does more harm than good as it enables the existing system to continue without fundamental long-term reform.

The second group of five papers examines in detail the progress of agricultural reforms, specifically land reform and privatization.

Soviet economist Elmira Krylatykh stresses that agricultural reform must be part of broader reforms, which include dismantling state control of the economy, multiple forms of property ownership (state, private, and cooperative), and the development of new free-market institutions. Agrarian reform should be shaped by the republics and be responsive to the needs of the farmers themselves.

Fellow Soviet economist Vera Matusevich examines the role of one of the new forms of ownership, the cooperative farm. Though cooperatives now produce only about one percent of total agricultural output, they are an important step in the transition from centrally controlled agriculture to more efficient, private farming. However, the development of cooperative farms will be slowed as long as many old-line bureaucrats oppose them as a threat to their power.

Gelii Shmelev, a Soviet specialist in private plots, argues that these plots are likely to be the main form of private agriculture for some time since privatization of state and collective farms will be a slow and costly process. These small plots produce about one-fourth of the country's agricultural output, primarily labor-intensive fruits and vegetables, but are limited by their dependence on state and collective farms for supplies.

Estonian economist Ivar Raig discusses that country's far-reaching efforts to privatize state farms and return property to its original owners. The state, during this transition to family farms and free-market institutions, has a central role in providing work for the rural population and in preserving and improving the land.

In the concluding paper of this group, Western specialist Barbara Severin cautions that land reform is only one of many reforms need to cure the ills of Soviet agriculture. In fact, immediate breakup of state and collective farms in favor of small private farms can only lead to more chaos and disarray. Consumer desires can't be met, she argues, unless efficient production is accompanied by a more efficient food delivery system.

The final two papers look at the role government and intermediary institutions, such as farmers' associations, play in encouraging agricultural reform and supporting the private sector.

American economist Allan Mustard notes that the Soviet government has traditionally controlled all aspects of the market, but that successful reform will require relinquishing such control, as well as privatization and the restructuring of production and distribution sectors. U.S. experience, such as tax policies that encourage investment, can be of great value to the Soviet Union during this transition.

In the final paper, political scientist Don Van Atta traces the mechanisms by which the central government and Communist Party controlled agriculture. He then looks at the role of new intermediary institutions, such as commodities exchanges and the Association of Peasant Farms and Agricultural Cooperatives of Russia, that are helping break the state's former control. These institutions have had little impact so far in changing the central control of agriculture. These new organizations, as well as agrocombines and agrofirms, can impede the development of markets, he warns, because of their monopoly positions.

The appendix contains the recommendations of three working groups in the following areas: improving the performance of the Soviet agricultural trading system; agribusiness strategies to enable Western firms to enter Soviet markets; and finance and investment strategies needed to speed the development of Soviet infrastructure and agrarian reform.

These papers and working group reports make clear that effective agrarian reform will require comprehensive, free-market reforms; market-driven prices; development of a distribution infrastructure and of commercial and financial institutions; and the breakup of inefficient state and collective farms. Efficient production, not increased production, is the answer.

New national and republic laws, new institutions, and prudent amounts of aid from the West are certainly part of the solution. Clear leadership from the top is also essential. But at its roots, the solution to the crisis is local. Real change must ultimately happen at the ground level in the fields, from individuals, families, cooperatives, and from invigorated state and collective farms.

In the short term, Western food aid may be necessary. But this aid should be channeled through emerging Soviet market mechanisms, new commodity exchanges, and nascent wholesale and retail trading networks.

And this food aid must be complemented by a sustained, multilateral effort to develop small, private, locally operated storage and food processing facilities; transportation companies, warehouses; and wholesale and retail sales networks.

But most important, U.S. government and industry must develop long-term training and technical cooperation programs and people-to-people exchanges and expand the existing handful of programs a thousand-fold. The West does not have the resources to fund the overhaul of Soviet agriculture. Western know-how and technology, however, can help create an efficient and profitable Soviet agricultural system, a system that can pay its own way.

Correcting the distortions of 60 years of misguided agricultural and economic policies will not, as we are witnessing today, be easy. The ailments of the former Soviet Union cannot be cured in 500 days or two years or three years. The process will take decades. But free-market agrarian reforms that put food on the table can be the linchpin for economic reform throughout the system.

> Michael P. Claudon
> President
> Geonomics Institute

P.S. The dizzying pace of change in the Soviet Union has continued since our October seminar. In December, the Soviet Union officially died with the creation of the Commonwealth of Independent States. The eleven founding members (Georgia and the Baltics did not join) are now struggling to determine just what they can agree on — defense policy, monetary and economic reform, price controls, and trade policy.

In late December, President Yeltsin ordered, in a sweeping land privatization decree, that state and collective farm managers quickly develop reorganization plans that would turn land over to peasants.

These are helpful steps, but they are no magic wand. The former Soviet Union and the new Commonwealth have a long, and let us hope fruitful, journey ahead.

Looking Beyond Production: What Prevents Soviet Crops From Reaching the People?

John J. Cavanaugh

All I see is that we don't know how to cultivate the land and that our system of agriculture in the serf-days was by no means too high, but too low. We have no machinery, no good stock, no proper supervision; we don't even know how to keep accounts. Ask any landowner — he won't be able to tell you what crop's profitable and what is not.

Leo Tolstoy, *Anna Karenina,* 1876

The winter of 1991-92 promises to be the Valley Forge of the Second Russian Revolution. When I left Moscow last Friday (October 9) having spent five of the last 10 weeks in the republics of the Soviet Union, trees near Tula were half-shed, and the smell of frost in the still warm morning air was clear and crisp. The Russian winter is fast approaching, and with it a sense of foreboding that this time it will bring with it a blizzard of social unrest, political turmoil, and economic paralysis. After five years of dramatic and peaceful political evolution culminating in the collapse of the Communist system which had ruled the people of the Soviet Union since 1917, the future of those new republics is shrouded by the coming snows.

We can view the Soviet Union today with both hope and worry. Certainly, the results of this year's harvest and this year's economic performance are daunting. The 1991 grain harvest is estimated to be 190 million tons, compared with 235 million tons last year. The smaller harvest has been accompanied by an even larger collapse in the gross national product from a negative growth of four percent last year to a possible negative growth of 15 percent in 1991. Oil production continues to fall, following four years of declining production at five percent per year. Production is expected to fall an additional 10 percent this year. And it is now being reported that two-thirds of the gold reserves of the Soviet Union have been sold into the world market.

No sooner had the tanks of the coup withdrawn from Moscow than these chilling realities began to descend upon the triumphant democrats.

As we describe the dangers, seek the opportunities, and chart the routes to the future, we should do so rea-listically and with our self-interest in mind.

Since Mikhail Gorbachev came to power in March 1985, our world has been transformed from one where a cataclysmic, nuclear confrontation between two military superpowers was a continuing probability into a world where a peaceful and productive, global economic system is a possibility for the first time.

However, the dramatic social, economic, and political changes of perestroika will not be concluded quickly, clearly, or without turmoil. The American Revolution did not begin on July 4, 1776, but resulted from the complex transformation of American colonial aspirations. These aspirations preceded the Declaration of Independence and the American Revolution and did not end with the surrender of the British at Yorktown in 1781, but required another nine years of political struggle before the Constitution was written and the Union formed in 1789. In all, the American Revolution was a 25-year process, and it is not unreasonable to expect that perestroika, which is far more complex, will be at least as long.

As the emerging republics seek to find their way to a stable, democratic, and market-economy society, their ability to feed their people will, to a large extent, determine the outcome of this unique historical opportunity.

What Should the West Do?

This winter will again test the endurance of the Soviet people, and the resolve and commitment of the West. Without question, the people face deepening and continuing hardships. What is not so clear is how best the West can help and, for us, what role the United States should play through its public and private sectors. The central government of the Soviet Union has defined the immediate need to be $14 billion in food, medical supplies, and consumer goods to survive the next six months. While there is no doubt the Soviet Union could easily absorb this high level of assistance, it is doubtful the assistance could be delivered without large-scale losses and corruption and even more doubtful that the overall effects of providing such a level of assistance through existing state-run distribution systems would be constructive.

It appears that the $14-billion-assistance request is motivated by a desire of the central government leadership to provide more than mere subsistence through the winter. The goal, expressed by some, is to provide a "democracy dividend" which will lift spirits, provide motivation, and provide immediate political dividends for the current leadership. As desirable as these goals may be, they do not appear to be realistic now or, it could be argued, desirable.

The more appropriate course for the West is a coordinated food, medical, and consumer goods assistance program to meet essential needs. However, this program should not be so large that it creates distortions or false hopes.

Even more urgent than this direct assistance, however, is the need for technical help in the implementation of a comprehensive and coherent, market-economy system. Falling production and productivity will not be reversed until the collapsed Communist economy is replaced with an incentive-driven economy. The longer the current policy paralysis continues, the more severe the economic collapse will become.

Almost immediately following the coup, the victorious democratic forces split into at least two distinct factions, the "populists" and the "undertakers." Both are committed to the establishment of a democratic, market economy system. The "populists" wish to proceed more slowly, maintaining large-scale consumer and production subsidies to ease the pain while the "undertakers" espouse an immediate transition to private ownership of production and market prices.

Many Factors Keep Crops from the People

Soviet crops don't reach the people today due to a deadly combination of inadequate production and massive losses caused by inadequate harvests, storage, transportation, processing equipment, and methods.

While the conditions which Tolstoy described in 1876 can be applied to today's conditions, the 1990 harvest of 235 million tons demonstrated that the production potential for self-sufficiency does exist. This year's harvest disaster demonstrates that this potential cannot be consistently achieved without stable management systems. What happens in the next several months in the economic reorganization of the Soviet Union will have both immediate and long-term consequences for the food supplies of Russia and the other republics.

The first concern must be the agricultural inputs industry. It is of primary importance that the centrally controlled agricultural fertilizer, herbicide, and pesticide monopolies be restructured to assure a competitive, market-driven supply system. A major factor in this year's production breakdown was the failure of these monopolies to meet farm needs.

Second, constructing a new Soviet food industry will require an orderly evolution of ownership of agricultural production from state and collective farms to various forms of private ownership and joint equity ownership. A comprehensive, new infrastructure encompassing such areas as fuel, feed, seed and equipment supplies, herd building, banking and credit support, and wholesale and retail product outlets will be needed to support private farms.

The third, and I believe the most crucial, element is the development of the food-processing industry. This cannot be accomplished without major investment and active participation of Western food-processing companies in the management, development, and even the planning of the modernization of the Soviet food-processing industry.

The fourth key element is the development of a new, food distribution system at both the wholesale and retail levels to replace the collapsing state system and the brutally corrupt black market.

The devil is in the details. I would like to suggest some of the elements of a successful program.

First, America has much more to offer the process of economic and political reform in the Soviet Union than we have contributed so far. It is critical that United States economic policy toward the Soviet Union be harmonized with the new political realities and recognize the enormous political and economic courage of the Russian people and the people of the other Soviet republics.

The United States must move beyond the single-minded policy of protecting and promoting the American-Soviet grain trade as the central driving factor of our economic relationship. We must develop a much broader and comprehensive policy which recognizes and promotes all of our economic interests including oil, telecommunications, timber and paper supplies, fisheries, and minerals, as well as the food industry. In each of these industries, American economic interests need to be asserted and promoted. America's future economic interest will be served by assuring access to both Soviet resources and Soviet markets.

American Food Industry's Role

The U.S. food industry has vital economic interests beyond supplying the deficit grain needs of the Soviet Union. The American food industry has the unique capacity to provide the new republics with the management, technology, and markets needed to raise the quality and quantity of food in the Soviet Union to world standards and to do it profitably.

I see four critical areas for United States government leadership. First, lead international financial organizations, such as the IMF, World Bank, and European Bank for Reconstruction and Development, in providing the necessary support for converting the ruble and stabilizing the Soviet monetary exchange and debt service.

Second, establish a comprehensive U.S.-Soviet trading system that includes export enhancement programs for U.S. technology and equipment sales, investment incentives, and guarantee programs.

Third, and perhaps most important, establish an extensive technical assistance and training exchange program at least on the same scale as the European Community Program, which this year and for each of the next three years with be funded at a level of 400 million ECU

Fourth, advise the Soviets on the type of reforms needed to produce a democratic, market-economy system.

The Soviets, for their part, must also take some immediate steps without which Western assistance will be withheld or wasted.

• First, conclude a union treaty that defines basic economic and political relationships between the republics and the central government.

• Second, adopt clear and consistent trade relationships for the movement of goods within the republics of the former Soviet Union.

• Third, implement immediate price decontrols and accelerate efforts to create a convertible ruble.

I believe that the long suffering of these people is nearing an end. A new era where a new and prosperous country will be built is beginning. During the next several days each of us will have an opportunity to define how we plan to participate in this process.

2

Overview of the Soviet Economy*

Keith Bush

We are in economic and, to some degree, political chaos.

Eduard Shevardnadze[1]

I am tempted to tell you the truth: nobody is in charge.

Aleksandr Yakovlev[2]

We are building mountains of laws, but no one is carrying them out.

Aleksandr Rutskoi[3]

At mid-November 1991, the Soviet state and the Soviet economy were in a state of considerable flux. What had previously been known as the Union of Soviet Socialist Republics was no more, but no agreement had been reached on the shape or nature of its replacement. Likewise, the world's leading command economy had disintegrated, its vertical and horizontal links severed, but the infrastructure and institutions of a market economy had not been created.

In the wake of the August coup and the subsequent dissolution of the compromised USSR Cabinet of Ministers, a caretaker government was established by presidential decree on August 24.[4] It was called the Committee for the Operational Management of the Economy, and it consisted of Ivan Silaev, Arkady Volsky, Yury Luzhkov, and Grigory Yavlinsky. In addition

---

Compiled on the basis of data received through November 14, 1991.

to the day-to-day running of the economy, it was charged with assembling a new permanent government team; drafting an economic union treaty that would delineate the boundaries and operation of a single economic space in a form acceptable to the members of any future union, federation, or confederation; and drawing up yet another program to get the economy out of its tailspin. It was expanded on August 28 to include republican representatives and observers from the Baltic states. Its authority was challenged by RSFSR President Boris Yeltsin on October 9, when he described the Committee as an "unconstitutional structure," and characterized its decisions as "mere recommendations."[5]

A decree of September 6 provided for what was intended to be the successor to the Committee for the Operational Management of the Economy. After considerable negotiation and debate, agreement was finally reached on its shape and competence. On November 4, Ivan Silaev outlined the structure of the new Interstate Economic Committee (IEA or MEK) to the USSR State Council.[6] The IEA is to be headed by Silaev, who was confirmed as USSR prime minister on November 14. It will be subordinated to an Assembly of the heads of the governments which have signed the Interstate Economic Community accord. The IEA will consist of five major sectors and 15 departments which will assume the role of the former all-union ministries. (Eighty all-union ministries and committees are to be abolished by November 15.) The IEA will retain control over communications, industrial safety regulations, power, and nuclear energy.

Economic Community Treaty Provides Framework

By November 14, all non-Baltic republics other than Georgia were reported to have signed or be prepared to sign the Treaty on an Economic Community — albeit with reservations and conditions. During its November 4 session, the USSR State Council told Grigory Yavlinsky to speed up the formation of the Economic Community.[7] The Council gave him one week to provide written proposals for implementing the 22 accords discussed by the 12 republics on October 18 in Alma Ata. Yavlinsky told the meeting that major differences still remained between republican and union leaders on basic issues such as taxation, servicing the Soviet foreign debt, and many aspects of banking. He said that some republics wrongly continued to believe that bilateral agreements can substitute for an economic community treaty.

In documents said to have been presented to the USSR State Council on November 13, Yavlinsky warned that the Soviet Union and its republics faced "final collapse" if they did not quickly agree to cooperate on banking, finance, prices, and foreign debt servicing.[8]

If it is signed and ratified by all or nearly all republics, the economic community treaty will be a step in the right direction. It provides for conformity in such crucial areas as the monetary and banking systems, labor market, capital market, transport, energy, information systems, taxation, and customs. It does not resolve such contentious issues as price decontrol and privatization. Many such crucial factors are apparently left to be worked out in enabling legislation and in interlocking agreements between consenting republics. Thus, although visitors to Moscow and potential benefactors are assured that the post-coup grouping has gotten its act together, as evidenced by the agreement to sign the Treaty of an Economic Community, the document is more of a framework declaration of intent that eschews murderous trade wars between the various republics. In any case, at this writing, it seems unlikely that Russia will wait for all of the republican legislatures to ratify the treaty.

In the meantime, there is really nobody in charge. Egor Gaidar, Russia's deputy prime minister in charge of economic policy, described the paradox succinctly: "The central government has the organizational structure but not the authority. The republics now have that political authority but no way of managing it."[9]

A Great Depression Ahead?

In terms of most salient indicators, the Soviet economy has been deteriorating rapidly. During the first half of 1991, when compared with the same period of 1990, GNP dropped by 10 percent, national income (produced) by 12 percent, and agricultural output by 11 percent (all in comparable prices).[10] For the whole of 1991, projections of GNP decline range from 13 to 20 percent.[11] A fall in output of this magnitude would sorely strain the social fabric of any country, especially one that has undergone the kind of political, economic, and social upheavals that the Soviet Union has during the past few years. It has been pointed out that the steepest annual fall in the U.S. GNP during the Great Depression was 14 percent.

In mid-September, it was predicted that the central government budget deficit for the whole year was expected to total 144 billion rubles, or more than 200 billion rubles if state bank credits were included.[12] On September 28, *Izvestiya* reported that the 200-billion ruble mark had been passed. The combined budget deficits of the republics were expected to rise to 125 billion rubles this year.[13] Thus the total budget deficit in 1991 could amount to over 20 percent of the GNP.

The money supply (cash plus demand and short-term deposits) was reported to have grown from 136 billion rubles in January 1991 to 236 billion rubles by the end of July, and was expected to more than double by the end of the year.[14] The managing director of the USSR Gosbank's money supply department told *The Financial Times* of September 18 that the two state mints and two money printing centers were working round the clock, adding: "The only limit to the money supply in the Soviet Union today is the capacity of the money presses." By the end of September, 200-ruble notes were issued, while 500-ruble notes were scheduled to appear in December.[15]

No recent Goskomstat data on the rate of inflation appear to have been published, but both Oleg Ozherelyev (the president's economic adviser) and Grigory Yavlinsky put the rate in July and August at 2 percent a week.[16] For the month of September, Yavlinsky modified this to 2 to 3 percent a week (i.e., up to 465 percent on a yearly basis).[17] Most estimates put the retail price inflation for the whole of 1991 at over 200 percent. At this rate, the ruble seems destined to share the fate of the Reichsmark, although a USSR Gosbank deputy chairman rejected any comparison with Germany immediately after World War II on the grounds that the Soviet economy is now in far worse shape. Arnold Voilukov told *Trud* on October 1 that Germany then had financial reserves 16 times greater than its GNP, whereas the current Soviet reserves are roughly equivalent to its GNP.

Foreign Indebtedness Has Increased

The latest authoritative estimate of the USSR's total foreign indebtedness came from the chairman of the USSR Gosbank, Viktor Gerashchenko. On September 25, he told a news conference in Helsinki that the debt amounted to $68 billion, including some $3 billion in commercial arrears and another $4 billion borrowed directly from Western banks but secured by mortgages.[18] Gerashchenko reckoned that the indebtedness of the USSR might have to rise by a further $10 to $15 billion "while it sorts out its economic problems." In his opinion, this would not jeopardize the country's ability to service its debts. On November 11, Silaev was quoted as putting the foreign debt then at 47.2 billion convertible rubles or about $81 billion, but some doubt was expressed about the accuracy of this figure and the conversion rate to be applied to debt owed to East European countries.[19] Yavlinsky has repeatedly asserted that the management and repayment of the USSR's foreign debt will remain under a centralized authority.[20]

The country's debt-service ratio (debt service as a percentage share of commodity export earnings, plus sales of arms, gold, interest receipts, invisibles, and transfers) rose from an estimated 22 percent in 1988 to an estimated 28 percent in 1991.[21] This ratio would normally be considered quite manageable; indeed, it is more comfortable than the same indicator for many countries. However, past and potential creditors are concerned about the USSR's prospects for hard-currency earnings in the immediate future.

During recent years, the Soviet Union's principal exports to non-Communist countries have consisted of oil, natural gas, arms, gold, and machinery. Owing to the growing exhaustion of the most accessible and richest deposits, inadequate investment, poor maintenance, and the general disorganization of the economy, the production of oil has declined in the past few years and, with it, the net surplus of oil available for export. The volume of oil exports in 1991, for instance, is expected to be about one-half of the 1990 figure and may taper off to almost nothing in 1992. Although most of the Soviet oil exported now generates hard currency, the world price for oil has remained weak. The possibilities of expanding gas exports are constrained by existing pipeline networks; little, if any, is liquefied for sea transportation. The chances that Soviet arms exports could be maintained at their former high level or even increased have been diminished by the poor showing of Soviet hardware and weaponry during the Gulf War and by the dislocation of the defense industry. As for the gold reserves, Yavlinsky is sticking to his disputed estimate of around 240 tons,[22] worth about $3 billion at current world prices. A USSR Gosbank official challenged that figure,[23] but whatever the true figure is — and it must surely be disclosed soon to the IMF — Soviet gold reserves and production volumes were evidently far lower than had previously been thought. Finally, Soviet machinery exports are likely to find few buyers in an increasingly competitive world market.

Money Supply Has Increased Faster Than Goods

Contrary to appearances and to the perceptions of most of its citizens, the real per capita consumption of goods and services in the USSR rose, albeit slowly, during the first five years or so of the Gorbachev Administration. The apparent contradiction between increased production and sales of consumer goods, on the one hand, and empty shelves on the other, can be attributed to the fact that the money supply has increased much faster than the value and supply of goods and services and to widespread hoarding.

Official Soviet data on the increase in sales of goods and services have been overstated insofar as covert inflation in state retail store prices and overt inflation on the kolkhoz markets have pushed up unit prices. Conversely, the statistics understate trade turnover, because they do not capture the growing number of barter deals (e.g., two bottles of vodka for an electrical repair, or scarce theater tickets for equally scarce medicines). They do not accurately record the large volume of foodstuffs and soft goods channelled through workplaces and privileged institutions, nor do they attempt to measure activity on the black and grey (semi-legal) markets.

A substantial portion of the increased value of retail trade turnover is due to the renewed growth of sales of heavily taxed vodka and other liquor after the abortive anti-alcohol campaign of 1985–87; for instance, the retail price of 10.2 rubles for half a liter of vodka includes a turnover tax believed to be nearly 1,000 percent.

Contributing to consumer malaise has been the increasing freedom to travel enjoyed by ordinary Soviet citizens. They have been able to see for themselves the yawning gap between their own living standards and those of the West. The disruption in retail trade has also led to longer lines and to the allocation of more work and leisure time to hunting down everyday staples.

Official policy regarding the imports of consumer goods from hard-currency suppliers has fluctuated during the Gorbachev period. Imports were cut back in 1986 and 1987, even though the USSR's creditworthiness was still high, and again in late 1990 and early 1991, when former Prime Minister Valentin Pavlov ordered draconian reductions in non-essential imports in order to try to salvage the country's hard-currency balance of payments.

To be sure, some astonishingly consumer-friendly legislation has been recorded. For instance, a review of the USSR Supreme Soviet's activity in early 1991 lists a decree on the minimum consumer budget, a draft law on the indexation of incomes, and — *mirabile dictu* — a draft law on consumers' rights.[24] Just how such legislation will be implemented, and whether the necessary funding can be found in the light of the stupendous budget deficits, remains to be seen.

The steady if unspectacular rise in real incomes was reversed dramatically with the open retail price increases of April 2, 1991. The initial supplement of 60 rubles a month, paid out in advance to most workers, employees, and pensioners as compensation for the higher prices, did not fully offset the increases. A Western study calculated that the purchasing power of average incomes fell by 15 to 20 percent.[25] A Soviet study reckoned that "the actual purchasing power of the population has halved."[26] No authoritative or meaningful calculation of the impact of more recent price and wage movements upon real incomes has apparently been published.

If or when a central leadership, the head of a viable republic, or the leadership of an economic community of consenting republics bites the bullet and devises and undertakes a meaningful transition towards a market system, consumption is expected to deteriorate further. It will be hard to demand more belt tightening from such a deprived population. Among those who are well aware of the probable political and social consequences of reductions in living standards is Valery Burkov, an economic adviser to Boris Yeltsin. He has warned of the hardships that will confront the more vulnerable strata of the population, notably the pensioners, invalids, and the service personnel withdrawn from Eastern Europe.[27]

Yeltsin's Economic Reform Program

On October 28, RSFSR President Boris Yeltsin outlined his program of economic reform to the fifth session of the RSFSR Congress of People's Deputies in Moscow. His speech was carried live on television and radio, and the text was published that day by TASS. On November 1, the Congress voted 876–16 in support of the principles of the program and gave Yeltsin the expanded powers he had sought to carry out his plan. It also voted 787–56 to grant the president the authority to remove local officials and to appoint regional plenipotentiaries to execute his plans.[28] The implementation of the proposed measures remains to be worked out by Yeltsin and his government and must be approved by the RSFSR Supreme Soviet by January 1, 1992.[29]

Thus far, no detailed breakdown of Yeltsin's outline program appears to have been published, and key aides to the Russian president have subsequently qualified or even contradicted some of the principal features of his presentation. The salient provisions of Yeltsin's plan, as outlined in his speech to the RSFSR Congress of People's Deputies, are laid out below. The quotations are taken from the transcript of the live broadcast on Russian Television, commencing at 0800 GMT on October 28.

Market Pricing Will Be Painful

"The most painful measure is the unfreezing of prices in the current year. . . . To make a switch to market prices in one motion is a severe, forced, but necessary measure . . . . Everyone will find life harder for approximately six months. Then prices will fall and goods will begin to fill the market. By the autumn of 1992, as I promised before the elections, the economy will have stabilized and people's lives will gradually get better."

Clearly, Yeltsin was talking here about retail prices. Elsewhere, he spoke of the adverse terms of trade for Russia in its transactions with other republics, claiming that the RSFSR was losing 33 billion rubles a year as a result. In that case, he was evidently referring to wholesale prices. His remarks provoked an anxious reaction from Russian consumers, who stormed the stores to buy up what little was left in them, and earned the hostility of the other republics, which are faced with huge increases in the prices they pay for Russian raw materials and will be obliged to emulate or counter Russia's move to free prices.

Three days later, the chairman of the RSFSR State Committee for Prices, Vladimir Zverkhovsky, stated that he supported free prices but that Russia would continue to control the wholesale prices of major industrial commodities such as fuel and raw materials and of farm produce, in addition to the retail prices of essential foodstuffs, medicines, public utilities, municipal transport, and children's goods.[30] Later the same day, in interviews with TASS and Interfax, Yeltsin explained that the prices of items such as coal, oil, gas, fuel, milk, bread, salt, baby food, and vodka would continue to be regulated. Regulation does not, of course, rule out price increases. The Russian president went on to say that a decree on the liberalization of prices was ready and would be issued without warning to avoid panic buying. He had, however, already promised in his speech on October 28 that the salaries of teachers and doctors, old age pensions, and students' stipends would be raised to the level of the minimum wage one month prior to price liberalization. As regards the timing of the liberalization, Yeltsin hinted that this would be during the current year, but a key adviser told a Western news magazine that January 1 or February 1 were more likely dates,[31] and *Izvestiya* subsequently gave January 1 as the probable deadline.[32]

Estimates of the increases in retail prices to be expected after liberalization differ widely. Then RSFSR Economics Minister Evgeny Saburov reckoned that prices would not increase more than fourfold.[33] Egor Gaidar thought that they would merely double during the month after liberalization.[34] Others were less sanguine: some even believed that the retail prices of foodstuffs would increase by a factor of twenty-five.[35]

While an across-the-board, simultaneous freeing of prices would feature in most Western prescriptions for the ailing Soviet economy, this key proposal of Yeltsin's program has run into much opposition from influential domestic critics. The mayor of St. Petersburg, Anatoly Sobchak, spoke out against freeing prices before a meaningful land reform had been enacted and before a guaranteed supply of food had been arranged.[36] Russian State Secretary Gennady Burbulis said that prices should not be freed until privatization was well under way.[37] And Vladimir Zverkhovsky warned against any across-the-board, simultaneous freeing of prices, advocating a step-by-step liberalization.[38] The trade unions, both official and unofficial, have reacted indignantly, but they have yet to take any decisive action.

To protect the poorer strata of the population — Yeltsin reckons that 55 percent of all families are below the poverty level even before his projected price liberalization — a social safety net will be set up, to include soup kitchens, hospices, and special stores.

Whether Yeltsin was wise to reveal his intention of freeing prices — the most radical element of his reform program — in advance remains to be seen. A similar, but much less drastic, move by former USSR Prime Minister Nikolai Ryzhkov provoked panic buying and such a universal outcry that it was abandoned.

Wages Must Reflect Market Conditions

"Wage reform is planned before the end of this year. All restrictions on growth of personal wages and opportunities to earn honest money will be repealed.... regard the trade unions' demand for free-market wages for free-market prices to be just, with one addition: there should be free-market wages for free-market productivity."

In his speech on October 28, Yeltsin did not spell out his opposition to full indexation of wages and transfer payments to compensate for price increases, but he and his advisers had previously ruled out such a course as being a certain route to hyperinflation.

Yeltsin was somewhat vague about wage policy: "Our strategic goal is to bring the fixed incomes of workers in state-financed sectors gradually up to the standard of those of workers in the free-market sector of the economy." Then, in a piece of pure Thatcherism, he added: "The prime factor in social protection for the public during the reforms will be accelerated revival of economic activity, especially in production, rather than redistribution of what we already have."

Taxation

Yeltsin noted that the tax system is "distorted and poorly adapted to market conditions....There is huge confusion in taxes, which produces mass violations of tax discipline." He was not very specific about the remedy, except to say that "an effective and stable mechanism" must be in place by the end of 1992. Outside observers — and, notably, the IMF — have called for a broader and more neutral revenue base, a fairer system of personal taxation, and, above all, the modernization and computerization of tax collection procedures.

On November 9, Egor Gaidar told the congress of "Democratic Russia" that tax reforms were vital, or else "there will be a period of hyperinflation when no privatization or structural reforms will help."[39]

Budget Stabilization

The budget for next year provides for a substantial reduction in appropriations for the support of inefficient plants, for defense, and for the administrative apparatus. From November 1, Russia will cease to finance about 70 all-Union ministries and other central institutions, whose existence has not been agreed under the economic community treaty. We are ceasing the transfer of money to the Union stabilization fund....The deficit of the budget for 1992 must be virtually nil or minimal.

Here Yeltsin is on the side of the angels. Nobody would be opposed to a balanced budget, but the consequences of a rapid elimination of the budget deficit could be most painful. An overnight withdrawal of subsidies from loss-making enterprises could result in millions of unemployed. And how long after prices are freed will it take to establish which enterprises are profitable and which are loss-making? Similarly, the world is waiting for a speedy reduction in the Soviet Union's defense establishment, which currently absorbs somewhere between 15 percent and 30 percent of GNP. But there will not be suitable jobs or homes for most of the demobilized servicemen and for the laid-off defense industry workers. Another pledge made by Yeltsin that will find wide popular support is to halt Russian foreign aid to less developed countries. Yet, a day later, his acting minister of foreign economic relations, Gennady Filshin, announced that Russia would continue to invest in civil projects in other countries, and he put a price tag of over 10 billion hard-currency rubles on this assistance.[40]

The reaction to at least one of Yeltsin's budget-cutting proposals was prompt. On November 1, the heads of the eight republics involved in the

Interstate Economic Committee voted to close down 36 all-Union ministries
and 37 commissions and councils within two weeks, thereby cutting nearly
100,000 jobs. Other ministries, such as the Ministry of Civil Aviation and the
Ministry of the Merchant Marine, have been granted a stay of execution
until January 1, 1992.[41]

Banking and the Ruble

Yeltsin made it clear that Russia would participate in the central banking
structure proposed in the Economic Community treaty only if other
republics unambiguously dropped their plans to introduce their own
national currencies. Since Ukraine, Byelorussia, and Moldavia appear to be
definitely committed to their own currencies, and other republics are
reported to be toying with the idea, it looks as if the RSFSR will go ahead with
issuing its own rubles. On October 31, Yeltsin confirmed that the RSFSR was
indeed already making preparations to do so.[42]

Although the IMF and other external agencies have counseled against
a proliferation of national currencies within the USSR, it might be argued
that republican currencies could hardly fare worse than the current Soviet
ruble, which has been debased by the central printing presses, which are
operating 24 hours a day, seven days a week. By November 5, the free-market
rate for the ruble was reported to have fallen to 110 rubles to the dollar.[43]

At a meeting on October 31 with representatives of the Union of
Russian Towns, Yeltsin said that he had signed a draft resolution to found
a Russian state bank on the basis of USSR Gosbank.[44] He called the idea of
a Russian bank into which "all hard currency and gold will pass" a bold
decision but said that "at any moment, we in Russia can be undermined."
The next day, TASS reported that Yeltsin had changed his mind and
"renounced his intention" of transforming USSR Gosbank into a Russian
state bank. This followed discussions with Silaev. Western partners were
reported to be "seriously alarmed" by Yeltsin's original proposal.[45]

On November 2, Yeltsin's senior legal adviser, Sergei Shakhrai, said that
the Russian president was about to sign a decree, due to go into effect on
November 10, replacing the current three-tiered system of exchange rates
—official, commercial, and tourist—with a single rate to be set once a week
by the market. A text of the draft decree says that all Russians will be granted
the right to the "unlimited, unhindered purchase" of foreign currency at
banks and exchange points. It also adds that Russians will be able to open
personal accounts in convertible currency. The draft decree declares
invalid any USSR customs tariffs, currency regulations, and legislation that

are at variance with Russian law.[46] At this writing, however, the decree had not been published.

Privatization

"Priority will be given to what is called small-scale privatization of small and medium enterprises in the service sector, trade, industry, and transport . . . . We have a realistic chance of privatizing within three months up to 50 percent of small and medium enterprises in Russia — that is about 10,000 enterprises — and also incomplete construction works, which should raise about 100 billion rubles in revenue....Within two to three weeks, the main principles for the privatization of housing in Russia will be published."

As Yeltsin remarked, the debate on what and how to privatize has gone on "for an unforgivable length of time." Meanwhile, "the Party and state elite were actively engaged in their own types of privatization." Yeltsin also set a rigorous timetable for the division of state property between the republics, autonomous republics, oblasts, and krays, which is to be completed during November 1991.

During "the next few months," shares in the larger industrial enterprises will be issued. Initially, shares will be divided between the state and the employees of the respective factories. Subsequently, the state shares will be offered to the general public at market prices. Yeltsin did not stipulate the proportion of shares to be sold to the work force. Practice in other countries suggests that majority holdings of shares by the work collectives often lead to excessive expenditures on pay and current benefits to the detriment of investment.

As far as the operating environment of industrial enterprises is concerned, Yeltsin announced that "work is in progress on a package of resolutions for the commercialization of their work. This means minimum budget allocations and an orientation towards maximum profits with prices freely established." So far, so good. The IMF would approve. What the IMF might have reservations about is the apparent lack of provision for enterprises that could survive and even flourish after a relatively short period of protection while they are restructured and reoriented. It was not clear from Yeltsin's speech whether this period of grace would be granted.

Demonopolization

Given the high incidence of monopoly and oligopoly in Soviet industry, the complete freeing of prices could give these giant enterprises the opportunity to charge whatever they like for their products. Access to foreign competition has been severely limited by the shortage of hard currency and the administrative regulation of foreign trade transactions.

Yeltsin promised to combat monopolies by breaking up some of the giant enterprises into separate and smaller competing units, and also by creating new small and medium-size enterprises in the wake of privatization. By opening up foreign trade and moving toward a fully convertible currency, the intention is to allow foreign competitors to sell products for rubles, which are then used for investment within the RSFSR, and to permit the competition-based sale of export and import licenses for rubles. Details of these ambitious plans were not spelled out.

Agriculture

Loss-making kolkhozes and sovkhozes will be broken up, and their land will be transferred to private farmers and to those who wish to set up small and medium-size "peasant trust enterprises." Those kolkhozes and sovkhozes that are performing well will be allowed to continue operating. A massive boost for private farms is planned: the RSFSR budget for 1992 provides for 6.5 billion rubles in assistance, while 24,000 tractors, 22,000 trucks, and other equipment will be earmarked for the private sector. One hundred million dollars will be allocated for the purchase of agricultural machinery and trucks from the West. The downstream servicing of agriculture (the food chain) and, in particular, the supply and retail networks are to be privatized "for the coming winter" — that is, within a few weeks!

As in industry, the criterion for a profitable or unprofitable farm has yet to be established. At the current state purchase prices, most farms cannot cover their production costs. Indeed, that is one reason why so much grain and other produce is being withheld this year by farms. (The other main reason is that farms cannot purchase much with their rubles.) The difference between what the farms receive in the form of purchase prices for their output and their expenditures on prime inputs such as machinery, fuel, chemicals, and labor, has recently been put at about 80 billion rubles a year.[47] If prices are indeed freed and foreign competition is allowed, it is unclear just how many farms will be financially viable.

A vital plank in Yeltsin's manifesto appears to have been removed — at least temporarily — by his legislators. On October 31, the RSFSR Congress of People's Deputies upheld a delay of 10 years before land can be resold or repurchased.[48]

Conversion

The conversion of much of the huge military-industrial complex to produce a greater proportion of civilian goods has long been touted as a relatively painless panacea for all of the ills of the moribund command economy. Little progress has been made, and a great deal remains to be done. Large sums of money will have to be invested before any sizable peace dividend will be forthcoming.

Yeltsin's prescription for expediting the process — at least on the territory of the RSFSR, where most of the defense industry is located — is to set up a special committee charged with making a clear distinction between military and civilian production. He expects the first results to be already evident by the spring of 1992, especially in the production of machinery and equipment for private farms and for the processing and proper storage of agricultural produce. Yeltsin also promised to safeguard the scientific and research expertise that has accumulated in the defense sector.

Foreign Economic Activity

Yeltsin made it clear that Russia would act as an independent, sovereign entity in its relations with other nations: "We have ceased to be an adjunct to Union structures." He gave notice that the republic was seeking membership in the IMF, the World Bank, and the EBRD, and he appealed to these and to the developed nations for technical help and assistance. Acknowledging the key role of Western investment in any Russian recovery program, Yeltsin declared the republic's willingness to provide the necessary safeguards for foreign capital.

Yeltsin's remarks about projected changes in foreign trade operations were elaborated on by *Nezavisimaya gazeta*.[49] The most important planned change is the abolition of import and export taxes on all types of goods and services. The draft decree instructs the RSFSR Council of Ministers to repeal the license and quota system for the import and export of all goods, with the exception of a very narrow list. Yeltsin is proposing a veritable revolution, although much will depend on the size and scale of that "very narrow list."

Going It Alone?

In a key phrase toward the end of his speech, Yeltsin said: "We have no possibility of linking the reform timetable to the achievement of all-embracing interrepublican agreements on these questions."

It seems clear that the Russian president was referring to the Economic Community treaty, which by November 6 had been signed or agreed to in principle by eleven republics — that is, by all except Georgia.[50] By that same date, 13 of the 26 implementing agreements were said to be ready; of the remainder, three were judged to require "a lot more work."[51] Profound disagreements had been reported among the member republics on such key issues as the allocation of the internal and external debts; the size of republics' contributions to the central budget to fund what is left of the all-Union administration; and the contributions to a regional development fund. In its present form, the economic community treaty appears to be merely a statement of intent, with little in the way of binding commitments. Agreement on a meaningful common market or common economic space could take many months to achieve.

An indication of Russia's future course was provided on November 7, when Yeltsin named Egor Gaidar deputy prime minister in charge of economic policy.[52] In contrast to Grigory Yavlinsky, who has consistently argued for economic reform at the all-Union level, Gaidar has recently urged that "Russia must have its own monetary and fiscal policy, and its own bank . . . . We must now move to treating all other republics as sovereign states."[53]

At this stage, it looks as if Yeltsin, Gaidar, and their team have given up on the nascent economic community. Russia apparently intends to go it alone and to refuse to sell its marketable commodities to the other republics for funny money. If it succeeds, other republics will be obliged to follow its example. Ivan Silaev, who has been acting USSR prime minister since shortly after the August attempted coup, who was appointed USSR prime minister on November 14, and who has much to lose if Russia breaks away, has implicitly admitted as much. He praised the salient features of the Yeltsin program and declared that the RSFSR provisions for price liberalization and rapid privatization would encourage other republics to follow suit.[54]

Conclusion

From the sketchy outline provided on October 28 and from the meager elaborations that have been forthcoming since, it would appear that Yeltsin's program for the reform of the Russian economy is the most promising to have been offered during the Gorbachev Administration. It eschews gradualism and sets clearly defined, albeit very ambitious, dead-lines for implementation of some of its key provisions. It goes nearly all the way in liberalizing prices and wages. It promises to transform the way in which foreign trade is conducted, and it offers more immediate prospects than its many predecessors for internal and full convertibility of the ruble, or whatever currency Russia chooses to use.

At the same time, the subsequent statements of and contradictory positions adopted by key aides and officials create the distinct impression that the rescue program was thrown together very hastily and that many of its provisions were not thought through. This is especially true of the plans for freeing prices and for privatization. Perhaps Yeltsin's motto is: "*On s'engage, et puis on voit,*" a phrase that originated with Napoleon and was greatly used by Lenin. The program smacks of conversion imposed from above rather than providing a level playing field for free market initiative from below.

Yeltsin's own legislature has demonstrated its ability to veto or delay a key provision of the plan, and the entrenched bureaucracy will not accept its own elimination without a fight. What is most important, public reaction has so far been generally negative, and the situation will deteriorate rapidly unless Yeltsin can deliver on his promises.

Even if it is only partly implemented, the Yeltsin program would appear to strangle the Economic Community at birth unless the squabbling republics can settle their differences and, if Yeltsin's gamble pays off, regroup around the Russian model.

Footnotes

1. TASS, September 23, 1991.
2. Cited in *The Washington Post*, October 7, 1991.
3. TASS, October 8, 1991.
4. CTV1, August 24, 1991.
5. TASS, October 9, 1991.
6. TASS, November 4, 1991.
7. TASS, November 4, 1991.
8. Reuters, November 13, 1991.
9. Cited in *The Los Angeles Times*, September 23, 1991.
10. *Ekonomika i zhizn'*, No. 30, 1991, p. 2.
11. The figure of 13 percent is Grigory Yavlinsky's latest estimate (see *Ekonomika i zhizn'*, No. 45, 1991, p. 7), while that of 20 percent emanates from Anders Aslund (*The Christian Science Monitor*, October 23, 1991).
12. TASS, September 13, 1991.
13. *Ibid.*
14. Interfax, September 2, 1991.
15. Interfax, August 31, 1991.
16. TASS, September 18, 1991.
17. *Trud*, September 26, 1991.
18. AP, September 25, 1991.
19. *The Wall Street Journal*, November 12, 1991.
20. See, for instance, *Trud*, September 26, 1991.
21. Derived from *The Wall Street Journal*, March 12, 1990, and *The Financial Times*, September 5, 1991.
22. Reuter, November 13, 1991; cf. CTV, November 9, 1991.
23. AP, September 30, 1991.
24. *Izvestiya*, May 23, 1991.
25. CIA/DIA, "Beyond Perestroyka: The Soviet Economy in Crisis," May 14, 1991, p. 10.
26. APN, June 4, 1991.
27. *Die Presse*, September 7, 1991.
28. TASS, November 1, 1991.
29. Interfax, November 1, 1991.
30. TASS, October 31, 1991.
31. RSFSR State Secretary Gennady Burbulis in *Der Spiegel*, November 4, 1991.
32. *Izvestiya*, November 6, 1991.
33. *Moskovskiy komsomolets*, November 6, 1991.
34. Cited in *The Economist*, November 2, 1991.
35. *Moskovskiy komsomolets*, November 6, 1991.
36. Radio Mayak, November 8, 1991.
37. Cited in *The Financial Times*, November 2, 1991.
38. *Sovetskaya Rossiya*, November 1, 1991.

39. Reuters, November 9, 1991.
40. TASS, October 29, 1991.
41. TASS, November 1, 1991.
42. Interfax, October 31, 1991.
43. RIA, November 6, 1991.
44. TASS, October 31, 1991.
45. TASS, November 1, 1991.
46. Reuters, November 2, 1991.
47. *Pravda*, September 19, 1991; cf. *Sel'skaya zhizn'*, May 30, 1991.
48. Interfax, October 31, 1991.
49. *Nezavisimaya gazeta*, November 5, 1991.
50. TASS, November 6, 1991.
51. *Izvestiya*, November 6, 1991.
52. TASS, November 7, 1991.
53. Cited in *The Financial Times*, November 4, 1991.
54. TASS, October 29, 1991.

3

Reforming Soviet Agriculture:
The Situation Today

Vladimir Tikhonov

The economy of the Soviet Union has always presented very difficult puzzles for Western economists. And it has often been impossible to find answers. For example, every year the Soviet Union produces up to 80 million tons of potatoes, which is as much as is produced in the United States, China, and England together. But there still aren't enough potatoes. Gross harvests of grain fluctuate between 160 and 240 million tons. The Soviet Union consumes no more than 145 to 150 million tons of domestic grain every year for animal and human consumption, regardless of the gross yields. But every year, regardless of the domestic harvest, the Soviet Union purchases about 40 million tons of grain from foreign countries.

We produce enough grain; our shortages are caused by an extremely inefficient distribution system for raw foodstuffs, in general, and grain, in particular. I have thus always opposed importing grain for human consumption. I don't oppose importing high-energy, high-protein grain for animals that we can't grow in our climate.

In the coming months, the situation could become quite tragic. For the first time, we risk a complete deficit of grain for human consumption.

What happened? A centrally controlled system of food distribution still exists in the Soviet Union. In previous years, the state procured up to 70 million tons of grain internally and up to 40 million tons on the world market. Thus, the central government apparatus distributed approximately 110 million tons of grain to the various regions of the country.

Regions have no system for freely buying grain for their own needs and receive everything from the center. But in 1991 state and collective farms, upset with state prices, declared a boycott against state orders. Instead of 70 million tons, the state managed to procure only 32 million tons. Today the government is offering very high prices for grain. It even promises hard currency and consumer goods for excess production. But collective farms don't want to sell grain to the state anymore.

Why? Imagine that you're playing a game of black jack. Imagine that I get 21 points. I've won. Suddenly my fellow player pulls a paper out of his pocket and says, "Here, I have a decree from the USSR Council of Ministers. Starting today the game is 19 points." I have lost.

Collective farms know how the government changes the rules, and they don't trust the government. No agreements can be considered reliable. Agreements can be negotiated, but no one thinks about the possibility that it might be necessary to fulfill the agreement.

This year, I fear we won't be able to buy even 10 million tons on world markets because of our financial situation. Export of oil has declined 45 to 50 percent. It's impossible to increase our export of natural gas. We've ceased to trade in weapons, because there's no demand for them. Gold reserves are exhausted. Hard currency debts grow daily.

Optimists say that 20 million tons will be imported. But we need 40 million tons just for human consumption. Regions where it's impossible to grow grain may end up without supplies from the center.

Moreover, the slaughter of cattle has already begun because of insufficient supplies of forage grain. State poultry and pig enterprises will very quickly reduce their numbers of livestock.

At the same time that we have these shortages, collective and state farms have already accumulated not less than 140 million tons of grain. But they don't have the right to sell that grain on commodity exchanges that are now appearing. In Kazakhstan there is not less than eight million tons of excess wheat. Kazakh state and collective farms need to sell that wheat through the new commodity exchanges and at free prices. But the government of Kazakhstan categorically forbids wheat to be taken across the borders of the republic. No agreement will change President Nazarbayev's position; he is intent on selling that wheat at a later date for hard currency.

Those who know the history of our country will remember that the famine of 1921 happened when the grain harvest was only 10 to 11 percent less than the preceding years. Why? There was a ban on free grain trade, and grain didn't make it to areas, such as the Povolje region. The 1932 famine in the Ukraine was not due to a poor harvest, but because of a ban on grain trade and the forceful confiscation of grain. The same is the case today.

Is there a solution? Yes. We need to immediately dissolve the system of state-controlled, centralized food distribution and immediately legalize and stimulate free trade in all spheres. Collective and state farms must transfer to a system of free trade, selling wholesale through commodity exchanges, and in wholesale and retail markets at freely determined prices.

The government's attempt to prevent price increases is senseless. It's doomed. The great mistake of Gorbachev, Yeltsin (whom I greatly respect), and Silaev (the head of the new commission overseeing economic reform) is that they act as though they are in a museum where they can prevent price increases by administrative measures. That's impossible.

By my calculations, approximately 1.5 millions tons of grain have been sold on the new commodity exchanges. That's about three percent of all grain. The spring price was 900 rubles per ton. By summer the price was 1,250 rubles per ton. Now the price is around 2,000 rubles per ton. The reason is low supply and high demand, because of the government's ban on free grain trade.

Finally, there's an intermediate measure. Gorbachev and others have begun to understand that they must end the monopoly of state and collective farms and gradually but decisively transform them into a system of free and marketable peasant farms based on private ownership, including private ownership of land. Naturally it is necessary to have private enterprises coexisting with various forms of cooperative organizations. Such genuine agrarian reform that reduces the power of state and collective farms will take 8 to 12 years.

Government's New Economic Role

In the past, the government had two functions: to divide and to subtract. We now have to find a way to teach the government not to get involved in the economic activities of enterprises. But we also need government's help to correct our problems.

Without government help, no farmer or cooperative farmers will be able to cure the land of its poisonous chemicals and pesticides. Even the best, most fertile areas in Central Asia will take several years to clean up. Farmers do not have the millions needed to clean up the damage from the past 60 years.

Right now, we have a very primitive tax system, the fragments of a system. Taxes are not viewed as a way to regulate the market, but as an element of a feudal, fiscal policy. Private enterprise cannot grow when the tax system — border taxes, the presidential fund that takes hard currency earnings, republic, and local taxes — leaves entrepreneurs only a small part of their hard-currency profits. People who are educated and democratically oriented are in power, but they are incompetent in economic matters. So we need education and technical help from the West at the governmental and enterprise level to help us with our economic and agricultural problems.

As for the proposed new union treaty, I think it will be very narrow in its scope. The problem is that republics not only don't trust each other, but they are developing a social-psychological makeup which contains the embryo of antagonism. For too long national and ethnic relations were suppressed or assailed. Today, we are paying for the sins of our ancestors. Now many governments want to create their own currency and insulate themselves from the inflationary ruble. I am afraid that this will only complicate economic development and stability.

It will be a long time before necessary interregional economic ties will develop again. That will happen only if the republic leaders retreat from a belief in government economic monopoly. Unfortunately, that ideology is inbred in the leaders of the new states no less than it was in the old leaders. New people have come to power in the center and some of the localities. But the first political and economics measures adopted by the new leadership don't differ at all from traditional measures. One can only hope and believe.

People in power today must turn away from the ideology of state monopoly. There must be a decision to end the system of centralized procurement of meat, grain, and other products. If the state wants to feed the army and those who are in jail, then it can buy the 18 million tons of grain. Peasants should have the right to sell their grain freely on commodity exchanges. The state itself can buy grain on these exchanges. President Yeltsin understands the necessity of such a system, but is hindered in adopting that system by old bureaucrats who continue to hold power.

We face a long period of upheaval and only a gradual normalization of interrepublic relations where producers trade directly.

There is, I repeat, one path: permit peasants to engage in free trade under reasonable government oversight.

4

Potentials and Deadlocks in the Soviet Food Economy

Karl-Eugen Wädekin

It has by now become general knowledge that the food crisis in the USSR[1] is more one of distribution than of production and should therefore be primarily approached from the distribution side. Such an approach is basically correct but threatens to be too simplistic if no distinction is made between its short- and its long-term aspects and not enough attention is paid to the possible remedies in practice under given Soviet as well as post-Soviet conditions.

Up to the abortive coup d'etat of August 1991, opinions among the political leaders, as well as a broader public in the USSR, about the future of the country's agriculture were divided. Authoritative statements have not been made since then. Many believe that land reform is the means to overcome the food crisis. Various proposals for land reform have been debated. They range from merely paying the existing collective and state farms higher prices and granting them more managerial decision-making, to creating half-independent individual farming within those public farms, or to dissolving the unprofitable public farms and quickly setting up a sector of family farms which may or may not be able to fully own their land. The latter view possibly has gained ground since its opponents have been compromised by their support for the Peasants' Union. The Union represented the interests of state and collective farm managers and argued for a go-slow approach in developing family farms. Union chairman Vasily Starodubtsev was a member of the group of eight conspirators in the August coup and is now discredited.

Shortcomings in the supply of inputs, services and transport, storage, processing, and distribution (the upstream and downstream links of agriculture) were already recognized in the Food Program of May 1982, but effective measures were not taken in these areas. After 1985, agricultural reform was more or less left to that of the economy in general. While broad economic reform policies will not be discussed here, two things of paramount importance for the food sector have to be stated: Despite all the talk about introducing a market economy, one of its central elements, free wholesale trade, remained a dead letter. This made it easier for producers to raise their prices instead of rationalizing production. In addition, general reform measures weakened the centralized economic, as well as political, command system. This permitted, along with a continuing "soft budget" policy, prices and incomes to rise faster than labor and capital productivity. Under such inflation, market elements degenerated into the safeguarding of enterprise and local interests and the bartering of commodities. This was detrimental to the development of money-based markets. In the food sector, this meant increasing inequalities between regions of agrarian surpluses and those which have to rely on deliveries.

This paper will concentrate on the main factors causing the food crisis and suggest some remedies. It will also briefly discuss how Western aid, cooperation, and business can benefit the Soviet Union and the West.

The Main Factors of Crisis

Between 1987-89, Soviet agriculture produced an average 0.68 tonnes of grain (after the official adjustment for cleaning and drying) per head and imported another 0.115 tonnes (net). Deducting roughly eight percent for losses, Soviets had nearly 0.8 tonnes (net availability) per head. This resulted in a mediocre level of nutrition. During that same period the annual availability per head in the countries of the European Community (EC) was 0.5 tonnes (0.53 tonnes produced and 0.04 exported). This resulted in a high level of nutrition.

In 1990 the Soviets had a record harvest of about 237 million tonnes of grain, which resulted in 218 million tonnes after cleaning and drying. Three hundred million tonnes were intially reported to be ready for harvesting. The grain output of the 1991 drought year will possibly be no more than 160 million tonnes (after cleaning and drying). Averaging the two years, one arrives at an absolute level somewhat above that of 1987-89 per head. And still the world resounds: "Food crisis in the USSR!"

Grain is the most publicized, but not most important, example of the belief that Soviet agriculture, even with its low yields per acre, should be able to provide sufficient food. According to Food and Agriculture Organization (FAO) calculations, the Soviet diet— calories, proteins, animal and vegetable fats — is sufficient for physiological requirements.[2]

However, a distinction has to be made between primary output, availability after official adjustment for waste, and actual consumption. In Western countries, too, output per person is not tantamount to actual consumption. The USDA's Ed Cook has calculated that in the United States, actual consumption of meat is around 30 per cent below output.[3] The discrepancy in the USSR is obviously greater.

In the following table on Soviet consumption (kilograms per person) in 1989, the author has estimated the actual consumption. The "norms" are those recommended by Soviet nutritionists. For meat and fruit these recommendations are below the 1987-89 all-European average consumption, according to the FAO. Milk and vegetables are above.

	Output	Availability (official)	Actual Consumption	Recommended Norms-1980
Meat	70	67 (59)	43-47	70 (61-62)
Milk	377	363	275-285	434
Vegetables	100	95	65-70	146
Fruit	51.4	41	30-35	95

The availability and consumption figures include net imports, part of which is processed and is less subject to losses and waste. Official statistics provides figures on supply, not actual consumption. These figures are based on output, trade reports, and estimates of the producers' own consumption. Household polls are not mentioned as a source of information.[4]

Meat and meat products in parentheses exclude slaughter fats and edible byproducts. Milk and milk products figures are in the following milk equivalents, possibly 2.5 per cent butterfat content, and butter, which in 1990, was 5.5 kilograms. Vegetables and fruit have been recalculated in fresh equivalents — vegetables exclude potatoes, but include melons and other cucurbitaceae; fruit includes berries but only for output and includes non-processed grapes.[5]

The Soviet agri-food sector as a whole does not meet demand, as the political leaders of the country, Soviet citizens, and foreign observers tell us. The main reason for this seeming contradiction is not farm production, but inflationary excess demand and waste. These may be summarized in the following five points:

1. The greatest unsatisfied demand is for meat and milk products, vegetables, and fruit. Beyond the above tabulation, it is the prices on the legal free (so-called kolkhoz) markets which testify to this fact. According to

1989 statistics, these meat prices were almost three times higher than official prices in the state retail trade. Milk products were 4.43 times higher, and some vegetables were even higher.[6] This may be an official understatement, but one has to keep in mind that free prices differ greatly at the local level. Since 1989, the price rise has accelerated. After the rise of the state-fixed prices of April 2, 1991, meat prices had tripled again by June in one central Russian town and had quintipled in Moscow.

2. Problems with transport, storage, processing, and trade cause huge losses of food on the way from the farm gate to the consumer. Lack of good storage capacity on the farms and throughout the distribution system is a major problem. The Soviet railway system is rundown and overstrained, rural roads are in an unbelievably miserable shape in most parts of the country, refrigerated rail and trucks are lacking, machinery in the processing industry is obsolete and in bad shape. Apart from the losses visible in the preceding table, grain losses, excluding pre-harvest losses, are at least six to seven percent, possibly 10 percent in 1990 (after drying and cleaning), and are thought to be higher than those estimated by the USDA.[7]

3. The population's demand for food, which exceeds supply and physiological requirements, results from a monetary imbalance. Incomes are rising faster than the production of consumer goods, (including non-food goods), while prices for basic foods are still fixed or at least regulated. The Soviet statistical yearbook for 1989, in an unusually frank footnote, states that "the monetary incomes of the population rose 1.4 times faster than its expenditures for commodities and services." This excess of cash incomes amounted to 28 billion rubles in 1986 and rose to 61.8 billion in 1989. By 1990 total incomes rose another 16.9 percent, while the supply (in comparable prices) increased by only 0.9 percent for food commodities, by 9 percent for non-foods, and by 5.9 percent for paid services.[8] The consequences are accelerating inflation, widespread rationing in various forms, and expanding second-economy markets, whether illegal, semi-legal, or legal.

During 1986-1989 total incomes increased by 28.2 percent and food purchases by 13.5 percent, which implies an 0.4 income elasticity coefficient of the demand for all kinds of food. This is most likely higher for animal products, vegetables and fruit.[9] Moreover, the rural population, largely self-sufficient in food, is included in the underlying data, and for this reason the coefficient is understated for urban consumers.

The situation is exacerbated by the fact that supply and demand (incomes) vary greatly not only by regions of the vast country, with its underdeveloped transport and trade system, but also by social strata and groups because of the ingrained, non-commercial distribution system.

Coveted foods (and other goods) are more accessible to certain groups of the population than to others due to belonging or not belonging to the *nomenklatura* and also due to the place of work. A poll taken in 1989 showed that 9.2 percent of those surveyed acquired scarce commodities and services at their place of work.[10] By definition, these are employed people, who account for about 20 percent of the population. Therefore, the 9.2 percent finding (the poll's size and methodology were not specified) may well be an understatement. In addition, the poll found 7.1 percent who received unpaid or partly paid meals, probably many of them at kindergartens, educational institutions, nursing homes, vacation hostels, and other state-run, social service institutions.

4. The excess demand under inflation is closely related to an intensifying tendency towards regional and local autarky and is reinforced by national assertiveness. The procurement "state orders," which replaced the previous obligatory deliveries, are only being partly fulfilled. Farms and local and national authorities are increasingly exchanging food (meat in particular) for industrial goods (such as machines, building materials, and some consumer goods). Without reducing the overall available quantities, this slows the circulation of goods and reduces macroeconomic efficiency.

The quantities of food exchanged among Union republics do not seem great. Interregional transfers of grain are still a state secret, but much of the transfer is in meat, milk, and eggs fed to animals. In a net balance in ruble terms, those republics that "export" food within the USSR are the Ukraine, Byelorussia, the Baltic republics, Moldavia, and Transcaucasian Georgia.[11] The great intra-Soviet exporters of meat and meat products are the same, except for Georgia which exports almost exclusively vegetables and pre-served and fresh fruit, and Moldavia, whose top "exports" are fruits, vegetables, sugar, and vegetable oil. The main meat importers are Transcaucasia and the Central Asian republics of Uzbekistan, Tadzhikistan, and Turkmenia.

The net total for all republican transfers of meat was only 278,000 tonnes in 1989, or no more than 1.4 percent of overall Soviet meat production. This is far less than meat imports from abroad, most of which go to Moscow and Leningrad. For milk and milk products the percentage was negligible at 0.2 percent, with only the Baltics and Byelorussia exporting sizable quantities. It may be surprising that the Ukraine ranks second to Byelorussia and the Baltics, because it is so much larger and has better agroclimatic conditions. The Ukraine's position reflects the fact that its eastern part is heavily industrialized and consumes most of the surpluses of its other regions.

The net balance figure for meat is composed of 2.372 million tonnes of imports (of which 1.7 million tonnes from abroad go to the Russian republic) and 1.258 million tonnes of exports. Even so, this turnover (including the above mentioned 1.7 million tonnes) amounts to only one-fifth of domestic output. Four-fifths are produced and consumed within the republics. The situation is similar with milk. Imports, foreign plus domestic, roughly correspond to the "all-Union fund of agricultural products."[12] This fund in turn accounts for less than 20 percent of total state procurements of meat and milk, of which the majority remains within the republics.

Thus, as far as Union republics are concerned, the disruption of food transfer ties, also possible in a new political arrangement, will not be a major issue. However, things look different when it comes to provincial exchanges within the "Big Three," Russia, Ukraine, and Kazakhstan. The quantities for export and imports of provinces within each of the three republics are severalfold greater. Only a part of these cross the republican borders. Such data are available for the Ukraine in 1987.[13] During that year Ukrainian provinces "exported" 1.043 million tonnes of meat and "imported" 323,000 tonnes. The figures for the entire Ukraine were only 410.3 and 33.3 thousand tonnes.

For milk, the corresponding figures were 4.819 and 3.397 million tonnes compared with 1.264 million tonnes and 259.6 thousand tonnes. Breakdowns for Kazakhstan are not available, but for the Russian SFSR we have production and consumption data for 1985, 1988, and 1989, in addition to those quoted for 1987.[14] They reveal great transfers among provinces within that republic and also great differences of consumption levels among its provinces. The food product flows there are into the Moscow agglomeration from central provinces and southeast Russia plus flows from the vast areas on both sides of the middle Volga to other parts of the federation, particularly the European and Siberian north.

To the degree that the flows among provinces begin to fail, those that have to rely on supplies from elsewhere will be hurt the most. Within the RSFSR these are mainly located in European central and northern Russia, Siberia and the Soviet Far East. (The latter two probably profit from foreign imports, from overseas and Mongolia.) In 1988, they received from 75.5 percent (east Siberia) to 91.9 percent of their meat supplies and from 81.2 to 95.2 percent of their milk products out of the "state resources," which consists of all the quantities procured by state agencies; only the region north of the Caucasus provided slightly more than half of its meat consumption without these resources.[15] Self-supply of private as well as public producers and some legally free exchanges should not be forgotten in this context.

5. The low productivity of animals is a central issue. Improving animal productivity — not even to the "best Western" level — would make most Soviet grain imports unnecessary.[16] While the pre-harvest losses of crops are not visible statistically, since only harvested quantities are reported, the on-farm shortfalls in animal production are mirrored in the final output per animal. The average annual milk yield per cow is only 2,900 kgs (6,400 pounds). An estimated 209 million pigs held during 1989 at various times produced only 6.7 million tonnes of pork, slaughter weight. That is 32 kgs (71 pounds) per pig per year. These low figures stem from long fattening periods of more than one year due to low quality and insufficient quantity of feed, bad pigsties, negligent tending, and epizootic deaths, among other factors.[17]

End-of-year herd numbers hide this fact. They speak of 68 kgs slaughter weight beef for horned cattle and 80 kgs pork for pigs, both per year, which also is dismayingly low. The pigs are sold to the state at 117 kgs, live weight, which by Soviet practice would be 80 to 85 kgs slaughter weight. Horned cattle are sold at 388 kgs, live weight, hardly more than 220 kgs slaughter weight.[18] So even the Soviet data reveal a fattening period of more than one year for pigs and of 2.5 to 3 years for beef cattle.

The poor quality and quantity of feed is reflected in the following statistics. In 1987, one unit of pork received 8.1 grain (oats) units; 13.0 units for beef and 1.48 for milk. Even this was an improvement over the years 1980-1985.[19] The low, feed- energy content of an oats unit works out to be the equivalent of roughly 0.85 barley units. This ratio is even less for low-quality protein and vitamin ingredients. Using good quality feed, the above feeding ratios would work out to be 5 to 6, 8.5 to 9 and 1.04 feed units, respectively, per unit of output. Cattle were fed 27.5 oats units per year, which is equivalent to 18 to 19 good feed units. Thirty feed units is considered barely sufficient for high-yielding animals in the West.

Total cereals imports of the USSR amounted to 31.3 million tonnes in 1987. Of this, about 2.5 tonnes of barley units per tonne of pork, slaughter weight, could have been saved, which at a conservative estimate works out to be some 15 million tonnes. To this have to be added some 9 million tonnes for beef (taking into account that much non-grain feed is consumed by cattle) plus savings on broiler and egg production and some grain fed to milk cows. If, in addition, one assumes fewer losses of output in the downstream links of agriculture, the Soviet "grain problem" will disappear.

No Quick Remedies

Changes in the food policy may be in the offing after the events of August 1991 and the proclamation of more radical reform, but it is not possible to discern the concrete steps, which are mainly occurring at republican levels. Recent experience in Poland, Czechoslovakia, and eastern Germany suggests that genuine improvements are not possible in one stroke. In the short run, reforms aggravate problems and hurt more vulnerable segments of the population. This is especially true in the Soviet Union with its vast territory and great regional differences.

Unmet consumer needs and the low productivity of animals may be partly remedied by agrarian reform. Better incentives for workers and better organization of workers into small groups within the big public farms may have some quick, though not sufficient, benefits. Nonetheless, for the foreseeable future, economies of scale will be very limited in livestock, vegetable, and fruit production. These are highly labor-intensive branches in Soviet agriculture, and appropriate machinery will not immediately be available. Training farm workers will also take time.

Creating private farms, whether family or corporate, is another remedy. But establishing large numbers of viable farms will require much capital and working skills that were killed in the collective and state farms. A changed economic environment geared to small- to medium-scale farming is indispensable. But Soviet industry has to learn to produce appropriate inputs, and this takes time. More important are the downstream links. Without at least partial privatization of marketing, processing, and other downstream links, small- and medium-scale family farms are doomed. This is especially true of new modern farms, which will require adequate inputs, services, and marketing outlets.

The process of setting up private family farms began in 1990. Most are of a primitive type. They might, for the time being, be able to compete with inefficient large public farms, and they might play a certain role in local markets, particularly for animal products, vegetables, and fruit. Yet the contribution of such farms in alleviating the food crisis will be very limited. According to Soviet reports, there were 47,000 family and kinship farms in the whole Soviet Union in the spring of 1991. The average size was 22 hectares (55 acres), and the investment in them, as most often mentioned in the press, was below 50,000 rubles per farm. The one billion rubles allocated in support of these farms by the Russian Federation government in the spring of 1991 works out to be 35,000 rubles for each of the 29,000 farms in Russia. This amount will be reduced as more farms come into being. Such undercapitalized farms can hardly be viable in the long term and are likely to become more of a burden than an asset in modernizing Soviet farming.

For the family farms to be viable, an investment of 250,000 rubles and more than 50 hectares (125 acres) of land per farm seems a minimum requirement. If 200,000 such farms are established, they will cost 50 billion rubles and cover about 10 million hectares. This is less than five percent of all arable land and less than two percent of total agricultural land. Such a private-farm sector undoubtedly would have a productivity potential which is high by Soviet standards. But implementation will require a few years. In order to make a real impact, at least a million such farms on roughly one-fourth of the arable land will be necessary. The cost of such conversion will become prohibitive. The point is that privatization will not immediately increase agricultural production. Creating family farms in deed, not just name, will require a decade. There will, however, be gains during this period.

A mixed, agrarian sector of small, medium, and large farms, of family, corporation, and cooperative farms may be the optimum solution. Most likely, competition among these sectors is likely to decisively improve the performance of Soviet agriculture. Cost reduction, which is already becoming a greater problem than increasing output, would be an important result. Yet this is a prospect for the long run.

Quick success is more likely in improving the downstream links, transportation, storage, and trading. Extensive investment is required there, too. It should initially be concentrated on storage and the processing industry. Investment in transport and trading infrastructure (including material supply procurement), which serve not only the food economy, received until recently a relatively small share of 12.2 percent of total investment.[20] The resources required for an increase would not seem to be an overproportionate burden. However, improving the infrastructure may have a sizable impact within a few years by diminishing the present huge losses. This investment could also turn out less costly than establishing even a small sector of viable private farms.

However, privatization, thought not necessarily complete privatization, is indispensable for efficent use of this investment.

Reform of the downstream links does not appear to have started. Establishing small to medium-sized processing plants on existing large-scale farms seems to be envisaged, and to have begun, as a substitute for more comprehensive investment. These plants are, however, essential in the future success of these farms.

Another approach is the formation of downstream cooperatives of private small farms, but this seems to be in a very initial stage at best. What is still missing is an understanding of the important role of private trade. There is ideological opposition to such trade, and it remains to be seen whether attitudes will change after the coup.

Balancing food demand and supply (point 3), requires more than reform of the agri-food sector. Reform must include radical currency reform and stabilization of the public budget. Without this reform, the change to a market economy is doomed to failure. There are no signs as yet that the Russian government under Boris Yeltsin, or the new all-Union state council, or the governments of the various federated republics are determined or able to reduce quickly state budget expenditures to the necessary degree.

Raising food prices alone, even freeing them from state interference, is a necessary but not sufficient part of a change to a market economy. It is questionable whether the government (or governments) can withstand the resulting social cost and political upheaval. Price rises needed to balance demand and supply in the food sector may even be greater than those in Poland, Czechoslovakia, and Hungary. In the USSR the overall food consumption level is lower. This implies that the price elasticity of demand is less and that diverting purchasing power towards non-food consumer goods is more difficult. Thus, continued rationing of various kinds seems inevitable and tends to perpetuate the privileged position of those who have access to food outside the general retail trade.

In this generally bleak picture, one positive fact should not be overlooked: The overall agricultural production is sufficient to provide food for all people at a level above minimum nutritional requirements. The case of grain was discussed earlier. Meat, another item of critical importance, also is in sufficient supply. Although this supply has declined somewhat during 1991, meat supply is comparable to that in Portugal. The situation is worse with vegetables and fruit, but this is exactly where private plots, including the gardens of urban people, can bring relief, and probably already have done so. Private plots, however, are labor intensive, and their goods do not reach all segments of society.

Priorities and Contribution of Western Partners

The most promising form of help and cooperation is training people: private peasants, extension service agents, organizers of new private and cooperative institutions of input supply, services, marketing, and credit, leaders of farmers' organizations, and public administrators. The benefits are both medium and long term. As this is an educational program, mentioning it will suffice in this paper.

Improving distribution should be the first priority in the short term. Comprehensive reform, however, will not be possible in a few months. For the very short term, Western food aid is necessary to help people through the winter of 1991-92. This aid would enable the Soviet authorities to spend some reserves during the winter with confidence that the reserves will be replenished for the period up to the 1992 harvest. There are limits, however, to the absorptive capacity of the Soviet food economy. Great quantities of grain accumulating at or near Soviet ports are of little help to people outside the metropolitan areas of northwest and central Russia, and, in particular, outside the metropolitan areas of Moscow and St. Petersburg. Last year's German food aid, for example, did not penetrate to a great extent beyond these metropolitan areas.

A glaring example of mixing humanitarian aid with domestic political issues occurred recently in Brussels when a representative of the all-Union government demanded that aid not to go to the republics as long as they have not agreed to contribute to a settlement of the all-Union foreign debt. There were also cases where Moscow authorities tried to prevent aid to Armenia for political reasons, or where the best restaurant in Kiev was named as a non-Moscow social institution in order to have priority in receiving canned meat. If Western aid comes to Moscow, some domestic supplies from the Caucasus north region or from Kazakhstan, originally destined for central Russian cities, could be redirected to Central Asia. Western control of shipments within the country and prevention of diversion by criminal organizations or local authorities may be helpful though far from fully effective.

Unfortunately, it is very difficult for Western official representatives to establish contacts with social organizations, which are independent from the state, such as the church in Poland or independent trade unions. Last year's cooperation between the Red Cross and KGB hardly served the purpose of developing independent and uncorrupted partners. Direct contacts with, and deliveries to, republican and local authorities may reduce losses from corruption, inefficiency, and waste.

It has to be emphasized by the Western side that not every domestic, private trade should be considered criminal. It is not trade but the attitude of Soviet authorities and citizens together with distorted and inflationary price structures that help illegal and criminal elements prosper.

Beyond this very short-term perspective, food aid will do more harm than good. It tends to enable the Soviet system to carry on without fundamental long-term change. Instead aid should be directed at improving the storage and transport facilities and at reconstructing and modernizing the food processing industry. This is an area where Western know-how can help, and where Western business can work with their Soviet counterparts. Western aid and technical help are only needed in improving the wholesale and retail trade network. Improving these networks, however, depends on the implementation of economic reforms, not just their proclamation.

The reshuffling of the administration after the August events appears to be proceeding on a large scale with the dismissal of many apparatchiks who sympathized with the putschists. If this is true, it will likely facilitate East-West cooperation.

Still, it remains to be seen whether such a process is really going on. The fact that all-Union property is being appropriated by the republics, that is by governments of a lower level, does not bode well. There is no certainty that the bureaucrats of the Russian Federation, or of the Ukraine, Georgia, or Lithuania, for that matter, will behave differently from the bureaucrats of the old, all-Union center and its local clientele. Communist administrative habits die hard as we have found in the German Democratic Republic.

Footnotes

1. For convenience, the post-Soviet federation, confederation, or commonwealth which does not yet have a name, will subsequently be called Soviet Union or USSR.
2. *FAO Yearbook Production,* vol. 43, 1989 (Rome, 1990), Tables 100-117.
3. Edward C. Cook, "A Brief Analysis of Meat Statistics in the U.S.S.R. and a Comparison with U.S. Meat Statistics," *CPE Agriculture Report,* U.S. Department of Agriculture, p. 33, January-February, 1990.
4. See *Statisticheskiy ezhegodnik stran-chlenov SEV 1989* (Moscow 1989), p. 452.
5. *Statisticheskiy ezhegodnik stran-chlenov SEV 1990* (Moscow 1990), pp. 411-412; *Narodnoye khozyaystvo SSSR v 1989 g.* (Moscow 1990), p. 118; S.V. Donskova, N. Ya. Ibragimova, *Ekonomiko pishchevoy promyshlennosti* (Moscow 1981), pp. 40-41.
6. *Sotsial'noye razvitiye SSSR 1989* (Moscow 1990), p. 170.
7. For estimates of losses and a description of the downstream links, both based on Soviet statements, see chapter VI of a forthcoming volume of the OECD.
8. *Narodnoye khozyaystvo SSSR v 1989 g.* (Moscow 1990), p. 76. The figures of this source for the "payments into the credit and finance system" do not seem to include the growth of savings deposits of the population, as they are less than the latter together with the direct income tax payments (*ibid.,* pp. 92 and 611). Thus 41.1 billion out of the 61.8 billion rubles cash excess of 1989 apparently were put into savings bank accounts, but this still leaves 20.7 billion rubles not finding commodities or services. For 1990, see *Ekonomika i zhizn',* no. 5, January 1991, p. 9.
9. Derived from by the figures in *Sotsial'noye.* op. cit., p. 139, including the higher prices on so-called kolkhoz markets. The income elasticity coefficient here says that if incomes rise by 1 ruble, the demand for a certain good (in this case food) rises by 0.4 rubles. This implies that for other goods (e.g., housing, clothing, cars, travel, or savings) demand will rise by correspondingly more than 1.
10. *Sotsial'noye,* op. cit., p. 211.
11. For these and the subsequent data, see *Sotsial'noye,* op. cit., pp. 152-160.
12. *Narodnoe khozyaistvo SSSR v 1989 g.,* p. 485. The all-Union fund consists of those state-procured agricultural products that are not consumed within the same republic, but distributed according to central orders (not necessarily shipped to and from the center).
13. *Razvitie agropromyshlennogo proizvodstva v SSSR* (Moscow 1989), pp. 165-179.
14. *Narodnoye khozyaistvo SSSR v 1989 g.* (Moscow 1990), pp. 96-100.
15. Paper of a Russian colleague, not yet published. Most, but not all, state procurement quantities go into the state resources.
16. An "advanced productivity level" broadly would be the Western level of the 1960s or so, depending on which country and what product you have in mind.
17. For this estimate, see K.E. Wädekin, "Seasonal Fluctuation in Livestock Numbers and Meat Procurements," *Report on the USSR* (RFE/RL Research Institute), vol. 3, no. 22 (May 31, 1991), pp. 4-6.

18 . Figures for 1988, *Agropromyshlennyy kompleks SSSR* (Moscow 1990), p. 80.

19. *Sel'skoye khozyaystvo SSSR*, Moscow 1988, p. 333.

20. On the 1986-89 average, see *Statisticheskiy ezhegodnik stran-chlenov SEV 1990*, (Moscow 1990), pp. 315-317.

5

Agrarian Reform in the USSR

Elmira N. Krylatykh

Most countries of the world go through an agrarian reform at some time in their history. Agrarian reforms reflect both the specific conditions of each country and common features of all agrarian reform. During this reform process, economic structures are changed, rural social problems are ameliorated, and modern technologies are introduced. Agrarian reforms in the post-war period in many countries have also redistributed land resources to the benefit of the peasantry, overcome remnants of feudal relations, and established individual farming. In the 1950s and 1960s, many agrarian transformations were caused by changes in technology.

The Soviet Union's agrarian sector has also undergone a variety of changes since Stalin's death. The method of planning production, purchasing agricultural products, the system of price formation, structure of state administration, and the forms of production organization have all changed over the years. But none of the resulting reconstructions touched the fundamental basis of the centrally planned agrarian order. Therefore, these changes should be called "reorganizations," a change in the forms of the existing system's particular parts without fundamentally changing the system itself.

The food crisis, which has become much worse in the last two to three years, is a result of deep contradictions based in the system of kolkhoz-sovkhoz production and strict state management of agriculture. The basic problem is that the kolkhoz peasant is not the owner or co-owner of the farm or its produce, so he is not interested in his work.

The only way out of the crisis is the transformation of the basic property relations in a manner that allows multiple forms of property ownership, (state, private, or cooperative), land tenure and economic incentives.

Therefore, by "agrarian reform," we mean that complex of measures which has already begun and will be carried out during the 1990s.

The General Conception of Agrarian Reform

Research institutions, legislators, and executive agencies of the republics and the Union are developing the basic principles of agrarian reform. This paper presents views worked out by a group led by myself and Academician Aleksandr Nikonov, one of the country's leading specialists in land reform. The fundamental goal of the reform is a stable, effective food complex, from agricultural inputs through production, processing, and marketing.

Three kinds of problems must be solved to achieve this goal.

1. Economic. This entails dismantling exclusive state management of the economy; ending state monopoly over property and land tenure; developing market institutions; and developing a new role for the state in regulating markets and economic policy making (tax, monetary, and fiscal policies).

2. Social. Here it is necessary to transform the conditions of life and work of the rural population and to substantially increase the living standards of all social groups.

3. Natural Resources. In this area, the focus is on the restoration, preservation, and improvement of agricultural resources, and implementation of resource-conserving production techniques.

The general principles of agrarian reform are: 1. land reform; 2. transformation of property relations and development of new management systems; 3. social transformation of the countryside; 4. development of agrarian sciences and new technologies; 5. creation of a market economy and development of regulatory structures; and 6. reallocation of investment in the agroindustrial complex.

There are four basic ways in which reform should be organized:

1. The socioeconomic features of the sovereign republics must be taken into account and reflected in the contents and instruments of the reform. For example, the tremendous socioeconomic differences between the Baltic states and Central Asia mean that agrarian reform is very different in the two areas.

2. Agrarian reform must be carried out simultaneously by democratic pressure from below and consistent state policy from above.

3. Agrarian reform must be considered an organic component of the broad socioeconomic transformation taking place in the country.

4. Proposed reforms must be objectively evaluated, both broadly, and

in terms of the results of each state of reform. This can be done with the help of foreign specialists and the dynamic adaptation of reform measures to changing conditions.

These four strategies are based on the analysis of other countries' experience with agrarian reform.

New legislation, organizational procedures, and regulations are also needed to transform the agrarian system. These mechanisms or policies are being developed by individual republics; they must coordinate their policies if the overall reform process is to succeed.

Land Reform

The essence of land reform involves the transition from exclusive state ownership of land toward multiple forms of property and land tenure, and the creation of administrative and economic systems needed to sustain a land market.

There is a legal basis for land reform in the USSR. This includes the Fundamentals of Legislation of the USSR and of individual republics on land adopted last year, republican land codes, laws on land reform, on peasant farmers' management, and various decrees of republican governments. Of definite significance is the decree of President Gorbachev on the primary principles of land reform. A number of republics have also created special organs for the conduct of land reform. Land commissions have been formed under the local Soviets of People's Deputies.

The first stage of land reform includes the creation of an inventory of land areas and their usage. District Soviets of People's Deputies can decide to remove land from collective and state farms in order to form special land funds. At the same time, the needs of new land owners must be clarified. Land can be redistributed in four ways:

1. The size of the private plots on collective farms can be increased. These plots would go to rural and small town citizens.

2. Land could be allotted to peasants' farms and smaller agricultural cooperatives for crop production.

3. Land could be allotted for garden and vegetable cooperatives.

4. Land could be allotted for home construction.

Preliminary estimates of the first half of 1991 show that 2,787 thousand hectares of agricultural area have been reallotted in all directions, including 7 percent for private plots, 57 percent in peasants' farms and smaller cooperatives, and 36 percent in garden and vegetable cooperatives. Nonetheless, the reallotted land represents only 0.5 percent of the amount of land areas held by collective and state farms. We forecast that in the near future this percentage will increase to between 8 to12 percent of the total.

The process of land reallotment varies from republic to republic. In Central Asia, the thrust of land reallotment is on transferring part of the collective and state farm lands to private plots to the rural population. In the Baltic states, these plots are given to farmers. In Georgia and Armenia smaller peasant farms are formed out of the lands of liquidated collective farms. In Armenia, land plots are sold.

The state will regulate land relations through the introduction of a land tax. Tax rates differ depending on land quality and location and vary widely from republic to republic.

We estimate that taxes on agricultural lands will total 11 to .15 billion rubles a year. These funds will be used by local authorities to improve the land, to create infrastructure, and to continue the land transfer process.

The main problems associated with land reform in the next few years include:

1. Shortage of land in overpopulated areas;

2. Settlement of areas with relatively poor land;

3. Introduction of new regulations for land relations, such as taxes, incentives for conservation, and sanctions for environmental damage;

4. Development of a financial infrastructure, such as mortgages and land banks.

In all the republics, especially in labor surplus areas, resolving these questions will increase social tension. For instance, a city dweller who gets a farm may be greeted hostilely by the villagers, who may even burn down his house. In the Baltic states, for example, there is often great tension when former owners return for their land confiscated by the Soviet government. This is especially true of owners who have no intention of working the land.

Reform of Property and Management

The basic idea of agricultural privatization is to permit state and collective farm workers to own the means of production. (After 1929, all land, according to Soviet law, belonged to the State. Theoretically, the land belonged collectively to the people.) There are different approaches to privatization, but the essence of privatization is the right of farm workers or others to be a owner or part owner of land and property.

Labor shares, which can be inherited, give people the right to obtain part of each year's profit. When farms are liquidated, shares will be replaced by direct compensation by the government or other associations. If the worker quits the collective or state farm to set up his own farm, he may be able to take productive assets from his former farm.

In the course of agrarian reform, management structures will gradually change, and the production share of individual farms and smaller agricultural cooperatives will increase. Many forms of cooperatives will develop and in 5 to 7 years, private agriculture's share of production will equal the remaining state share.

Agrarian reform includes the creation of public works and social services, such as roads, health care, and schools. At present most rural districts of the RSFSR, Kazakhstan, and Central Asia are underdeveloped in terms of public health, education, and cultural institutions. There is also a great need for roads, transport, and routine services in many rural areas. The republics themselves develop social programs, which are financed through local budgets. Some areas are particularly depressed. For example, special problems exist in the areas that have suffered from the Chernobyl nuclear power plant failure, and great sums of money are needed to move and organize people in these areas of Russia, Byelorussia, and Ukraine.

Extensive technological changes will be needed in the course of agrarian reform. Most important is the need to establish complex mechanization and the need to use technology that does not contribute to environmental degradation. Currently there are about 100 local, scientific and technical programs and projects which seek to develop more efficient methods of food production.

Mastering Market Instruments and Creating a New Role for the State

The transition to a market economy is the most important component of agrarian reform and will help eliminate the monetary overhang. The volume of food production in 1990 was worth about 150 billion rubles in retail prices. Soviet consumers, however, had another 250 to 270 billion rubles to be spent on food and consumer goods had they been available. The April 1991 retail price hike, which pushed prices up 2 to 3 times, did not help to balance supply and demand or cure the monetary overhang. Although market prices increased, supplies in state outlets did not. Instead, we have seen a dangerous trend — a result of the ongoing political and economic chaos — pointing toward an absolute decrease in agriculture and industrial production for 1991.

Agrarian reform envisages the creation of an infrastructure for wholesale trade. The first commodity exchanges have already appeared in grain, agricultural machinery, and building materials. Cooperatives are also developing to procure and sell agricultural products and material and to provide technical support.

Creating the basic market infrastructure will take several years, and there will be an overlapping of the former administrative system and the new market system. A principal goal of agrarian reform policy should be to protect and encourage the development of these new market institutions.

The role of the state will change. Instead of directly influencing the production and distribution of commodities, the state will develop a new regulatory and economic policy-making role. It will set up a taxation system, subsidies, support prices, and anti-monopoly policies. At the present time, the legal basis is being created for this new state role.

Structural Shifts in the Agroindustrial Complex

Agrarian reform must also involve extensive infrastructural changes and improvements in harvesting, processing, distribution, transportation, and marketing. Under central planning, there have been huge losses of agricultural commodities and raw materials and very inefficient use of all resources. Without improved food processing and storage, all efforts to increase agricultural production will be useless. These structural problems further complicate the transition to a market economy. Ultimately, reforming the agroindustrial complex will require a joint effort of the central government, whatever its form, the individual republics, and private parties such as foreign investors.

Constructing and reconstructing food processing and storage enterprises and developing food processing equipment will require a tripling and quadrupling of investment in these areas in the next several years. Structural reconstruction will also require the accelerated development and demonopolization of the production of agricultural machinery, fertilizers, and pest control chemicals. In addition, substantial investment is needed in agrarian science to train personnel.

Agrarian reform in the USSR has entered its first phase. Its first tasks are to overcome the food crisis, fill shelves with food, and stabilize the financial situation of agrarian enterprises. The results of these tasks should be known by the end of 1992.

6

Cooperatives:
The Seeds of a Market Economy?

Vera Matusevich

Along with the death of the Soviet Union, we have been witnessing the collapse of the central government's command economy. As our centrally planned economy evolves toward some form of market economy, many new forms of economic organization are emerging.

Cooperatives are one of these forms. Historically, Soviet cooperatives have not been financially independent, self-managed cooperatives in the Western sense. Rather, like state enterprises, they have been totally reliant on the state planning system.

About 18 percent of the Soviet labor force of 164 million workers are involved in cooperatives; over 80 percent work for the state. But this first figure is misleading as the vast majority of these cooperative employees work on collective farms and consumer cooperatives, both of which are not true cooperatives. Only about four percent of the work force is involved in the new cooperatives.

Soviet cooperatives formed in the past several years are closer to the Western model, but they don't exist in a market environment and still must operate differently from Western cooperatives. In many cases, the first cooperatives were established to circumvent government restrictions and were not intended to be worker-run institutions. Many of the first cooperatives were set up by the "mafia" and charged exorbitant prices, compared to state prices, for scarce consumer goods. These cooperatives, which have created a new class of wealthy entrepreneurs, have angered many citizens and have frequently given cooperatives a bad name.

Nonetheless, "true" cooperatives are starting to emerge, such as those organized by private farmers. Private farmers and their agricultural cooperatives represent only one percent of agricultural production, but the cooperative movement has great potential. New cooperatives, made up of farmers, but also of workers in the supply, processing, distribution, and marketing sectors are essential if private farming and agricultural reform are to succeed. These new cooperatives can provide essential services during and after the transition from the single-source central economy to a diversified, more efficient market economy.

For the West, these new agricultural cooperatives, run by aggressive, innovative farmers, not by a central bureaucracy, can be the vehicle for joint ventures, investment, training programs, and trade.

The Destructive Legacy of "Cooperative' Collective Farms

Soviet leaders for ideological and political reasons have sometimes called collective farms, cooperative farms. But Soviet collective farms meet none of the conditions of true cooperatives and were created by Stalin to suppress and control independent peasant farmers.

Until Stalin's forced collectivization began in 1928, private peasant farms in the rural areas created cooperatives for marketing, supply, servicing, credit, and processing. Peasant farms were economically independent and reacted to market forces. In 1928, peasant farmers, protesting the lack of consumer goods and farm equipment and low, state grain payments, withheld their grain from the state. To break the independence of farmers and to squeeze the agriculture sector to fund heavy industrialization, Stalin began the forced collectivization of millions of small peasant farmers and the exile to Siberia of millions more.

The government declared that all land was property of the state. The personal property of the peasants was considered to be part of the of the collective. The state and party apparatus, not the collective farm member, made all decisions about the farm's operation.

Peasants could not feed their families on their fixed, collective farm salaries. Often the main source of income for the family was their private plot, an allotment of an acre or less, where they grew vegetables and raised animals. In 1989, only about two percent of the total farm land of collective farms was devoted to private plots, but these intensively cultivated plots created about 25 percent of total family income of collective farm members.

The destructive legacy of collectivization can be felt throughout Soviet agriculture today and will affect the development of cooperative farms. Collective farm workers received the same guaranteed state wage regardless of their productivity and output. This wage leveling reduced any incentive for workers to produce more or work harder. Today, workers accustomed to equal pay resent those who are wealthier, even when their wealth results from hard work. The psychology that everyone must be equally poor is a major hurdle.

Second, collective farm workers had almost no say in decision making. As a result, once-independent peasantry lost much of their interest in and ability to make decisions.

In essence, the country's 28,000 collective farms are hardly a model for today's cooperative farms. They are far larger — they average about 22,000 acres, have roughly 5,000 head of livestock, and 400-plus farm workers — than any likely cooperative farm arrangement. They are not user-owned, user-supported, or user-managed. However, they do produce about 35 to 40 percent of total agricultural output, about the same amount as state farms. Given the major obstacles in the transition to private farming, collective and state farms will continue to play a major role in Soviet agriculture.

Consumer "Cooperatives" Are a Misnomer

Consumer cooperatives were set up by industrial workers at the end of the 19th century to supply their members with consumer goods. However, during and after collectivization, the essence of these cooperatives was perverted, and they were transformed into a bureaucratically centralized system, no different from the state trading and procurement system. These cooperatives became part of the command system and did not operate democratically. After 1935, consumer cooperatives were allowed only in rural areas.

In reality, the system of consumer cooperatives turned into monopolies in the rural areas. Rural inhabitants had to pay more (7 to 15 percent) for poor goods allocated by planning bodies. There was no other seller. Sometimes the nearest shop was hundreds of miles away.

The 9,300 cooperatives served more than 60 million people and were responsible for more than one-quarter of all retail trade in the country. In rural areas, its share was more than 90 percent.

These cooperatives, with the help of local bosses, attempted to eliminate all trade and procurement competitors. Cooperatives grew because there were no other trading systems, but hired managers, not members, made the decisions.

By paying small or no dividends to members, underpaying suppliers, and overcharging for consumer goods, consumer cooperatives became one of the richest organizations in the Soviet Union, with multi-billion ruble properties. However, the members' share of those properties was only four percent. Who owns the other 96 percent is disputed. The Central and republic cooperative staffs claim they, not the 60 million cooperative members, own all real and movable property. They are, however, ready to share a small part of the property with three million hired workers — sellers, cooks, and procurement workers.

Cooperatives in the Perestroika Era

The Law on Cooperatives in 1988 created a new form of cooperative, cooperatives that mainly produced consumer goods and services. These cooperatives, which have produced desperately needed goods and services, if at high prices, have grown dramatically: from an output of 270 million rubles in 1987 to 70 billion rubles, about seven percent of the gross national product, in 1990.

These cooperatives are fully independent, self-supporting and a form of free enterprise. It is difficult to overestimate the role and importance of these cooperatives. First, they are the prototypes of new market structures. Even with an economic crisis, and the opposition of central government and local authorities, cooperatives have grown rapidly.

Second, these cooperatives have created a class of entrepreneurs and a new type of Soviet people. These resilient, innovative entrepreneurs have thrived despite the economic and bureaucratic obstacles that have often stymied American firms and entrepreneurs.

Third, cooperatives have created much-needed competition for state monopolies. Through these cooperatives, we are getting firsthand experience on decentralizing and demonopolizing our economy.

Fourth, cooperatives have proven to be more efficient than state enterprises and have disproved the economic postulate that bigger is better. Because of the cooperatives' success, ministries have had to weaken government restrictions, such as restrictive taxation, on them.

Fifth, cooperatives have prodded and supported democratic movements in the country.

Nevertheless, most new cooperatives still do not meet Western definitions of independent cooperatives. Entrepreneurs established "cooperatives," because there were no laws until the late 1980s permitting the creation of small businesses. First, most cooperatives have members/shareholders, who run the cooperative, and hired workers who are not members. Hired workers can make up 80 to 90 percent of the work force. This percentage has been dropping — hired workers now average about 40 percent of the work force — because of government limits on hired workers.

Second, more than half of the cooperatives are attached to state industrial enterprises and often do not have their own means of production, or the ability to operate freely. Only about 10 billion of the 70 billion rubles of cooperatives' gross output is available to the general public while the rest has been restricted to state enterprises.

Third, because of consumer goods shortages, cooperatives have sometimes become monopolies in their own right and have created artificially high prices. Cooperatives began the price spiral on consumer goods and have been a major factor in the inflation that now threatens to make the ruble worthless. These high prices have most antagonized people with low and middle incomes, who cannot buy their goods or services.

I can recall meeting an American businessman at a famous Moscow cooperative restaurant, Kropotkinskoe 34, with his girlfriend. I asked him the price of his dinner

"Not expensive, only $98," he answered.

At the time the average monthly salary was about 260 to 280 rubles, and he had spent the equivalent of more than 3,000 rubles.

"But there is no other place to eat a good meal," he explained, aware of my astonishment. "And the roses on the table are so beautiful."

Agricultural Cooperatives Can't Exist within Collectives

Since perestroika, there have been several attempts within state and collective farms to create more democratic organizations that have the economic size to be independent from the central bureaucracy. These organizations — lease brigades, agrocombinants, and agrofirms — represent more sophisticated forms of organizations and payment for labor, and, at their best, do have more flexibility in planning and marketing.

Agrocombinants integrated dozens of state and collective farm in a district with processing plants and marketing networks. However, the 280 combinats are run by a combinat council and leave little room for individual initiative.

Agrofirms, groups of collective farms that are most prevalent in the

Baltic states, are more vertically integrated organizations that join farms with transportation, processing, and retail operations. They aspire to operate more cooperatively, but collective farm regulations limit many progressive undertakings.

In the past few years, "semi-cooperatives" or lease brigades have been formed in the state and collective farms. As part of Gorbachev's agricultural reform program to encourage individual initiative and increase productivity, workers could lease, for nominal charges, land, buildings, materials, and equipment from their state and collective farms. At their best, brigades can decide what they will grow and where they will sell it. However, brigades remain dependent on the state and collective farms for land, seed, and machinery, and brigade members are more accurately sharecroppers than independent farmers.

Conservative collective and state farm managers have generally opposed the introduction of these alien bodies in their managerial domain, and it is unlikely that truly independent cooperatives can ever exist within the old collective and state farm system.

In an attempt to offset the still formidable powers of conservative managers and the central bureaucracy, cooperatives have formed regional agroindustrial associations. These umbrella organizations attempt to represent the interests of all parts of the agricultural sector: independent farmers, suppliers, processors, builders, marketers. The association is run by a council of elected representatives from the different organizations.

True Agricultural Cooperatives Are Emerging

True agricultural cooperatives are beginning to emerge as part of the wider cooperative movement that has spread rapidly in consumer goods and services in recent years. The production of these new agricultural cooperatives is still small, about one percent of the total agricultural output, but they have proven to be more efficient and innovative than state and collective farms.

Some of these new agricultural cooperatives have been created by the breakup of collective farms into agricultural partnerships. Others have been organized by groups of people who received land from local authorities or leased it from the state or collective farms. Other cooperatives or associations are being organized by emerging private farmers.

Yeltsin's decree on land privatization, issued December 1991, is a radical and needed step to speed the division of state and collective farms. Initial land reform decrees did not resolve the problem of land ownership. Farmers did not own the land and couldn't mortgage their property to get desperately needed bank loans. Farmers who did receive land frequently received marginal or poor land at best. Yeltsin's order, effective March 1, will begin to change all this.

Collective and state farm workers can freely withdraw from the farm and receive a fair share of land. They will have the right to buy, sell, trade or mortgage property for the first time. In essence, the decree will create a free market in land.

Collective and state farm managers must develop reorganization plans to turn over land to individual farmers by March 1 or face heavy fines. Reorganization is no longer a matter of choice; managers will no longer be able to prevent the creation of private farms.

However, Yeltsin's decree does not resolve one of the major hurdles in the development of private farming — the lack of a supply and marketing system. Creating marketing, supply, and service cooperatives is the number one task for private farmers. Private farmers — there were 41,000 private farms at the beginning of 1991 — are trying to organize lobbying organizations. In practically every region there are local associations of private farmers. Local associations are affiliated into regional ones, and then into republican associations. In Russia, the umbrella organization for all such farm organizations is the Association of Peasants' Farms and Farmers' Cooperatives (AKKOR).

The Union of Amalgamated Cooperatives serves a similar lobbying and coordinating function for the entire cooperative movement in services, consumer goods, and agriculture.

Some critics of these new associations contend that these groups also need competing associations if they are not to become as dictatorial as the former central ministries.

Soviet Cooperatives Differ from American Ones

The fledgling Soviet cooperative movement has been less concerned with the traditional objectives of cooperatives: self-management and democratic governance, economic independence, consolidation to create political and economic bargaining power.

For many, Soviet cooperatives are an economic way station in the transition from near total state ownership of the means of production to private business and private property. Many leaders of the "new" cooperatives are not interested in and reject the philosophy that cooperatives are voluntary unions to achieve social and economic goals. But without these goals, real cooperatives are impossible.

Until now, Soviet cooperatives have been considered a special form of property, different from private and state ownership. But cooperatives will require the private land ownership that Yeltsin's decree provides, if members are to be economically independent. We cannot continue to play semantic games for ideological reasons. There is either state or private land ownership. Everything else is a variation of these two basic forms.

In the United States cooperatives are respected, strong businesses. In the Soviet Union, cooperatives are secondary businesses, mostly small or agriculturally based. Many cooperatives have also been shadowy businesses run by a new breed of profiteering speculators. However, we must realize that the cooperatives' excesses are more a reflection of the country's political and economic chaos and are not inherent defects. True cooperatives that are democratically run and encourage competition can play a vital role in the economic reform of the Soviet Union.

Most American agricultural cooperatives have been set up to improve the purchasing power, distribution and marketing of produce of economically independent farms; they are not production cooperatives. American farmers may belong to several cooperatives: a telephone cooperative, a marketing cooperative for his milk, a farm supplies cooperative.

Compared to the United States, the former Soviet Union has a high percentage of production cooperatives. In 1989, consumer goods and services cooperatives made up 20 and 25 percent, respectively, of the newly formed cooperatives. In general, these cooperatives were formed to quickly and profitably meet the enormous, unmet demands of Soviet consumers. Agricultural cooperatives, which made up only three percent of the new cooperatives, cannot reap such immediate profits but must be concerned with long-term development of the agricultural infrastructure if they are to survive.

In the first years of perestroika, cooperatives were seen as a major element in economic restructuring. But by 1989, this initial enthusiasm had passed, a victim of the cooperatives' excesses on the one hand and the resistance of the bureaucracy on the other. Today, it is possible to come to a more balanced view of their advantages and disadvantages.

True Cooperatives Must be Encouraged

First, we need a clear economic reform program and an effective strategy for the development of cooperatives.

During the past two years, nearly a dozen different reform programs have been debated. Yeltsin's economic reform program, supported by Russia's Congress in November 1991, promises to be a good start for real reform. The Yeltsin Plan encompasses privatization, demonopolization, price liberalization, budget stabilization, a financial boost for private farms, and the privatization of the supply and retail network servicing agriculture. This plan will create much needed wholesale and retail markets and end the state procurement policy of mandatory orders, the policy which has created today's food crisis.

Yeltsin's plan will create a market environment and make it possible to develop self-managed cooperatives. With independence, cooperative members will have the financial incentive to develop the managerial, production, and distribution skills needed to succeed in a market economy.

State and collective farms, long used to orders from the center, can never be as responsive to the market as cooperatives and private farms. A new system that encourages the individual is needed to break the bad habits of 60 years of central control. In the short term, productive, technologically advanced state and collective farms should not be dismantled. To do so would only exacerbate existing food production and distribution problems.

But in the long term, there must be radical economic change inside such collective farms. Loss-making collective farms must be broken up and their land transferred to private farmers. Profitable collectives can be turned into shareholding enterprises or collectives. Yeltsin's plan should speed this process.

In the Soviet Union, after four generations of forced collectivization, we have lost our tradition of private farming. That is why it is better to awaken people's interests and initiative using radical economic methods. It means that collective farms can be used as distribution and collection channels, or like Western marketing and supply cooperatives after collective farmers become independent producers.

Independent farmers from the transformed collectives could voluntarily join small production cooperatives. These self-supporting mini-cooperatives could then assign some marketing or supply functions to the former administration of collectives. Former collective managers would then become partners of producers and their mini-cooperatives.

Such a system could be effective if private farmers or their small productive cooperatives had the opportunity to develop competing cooperatives. Demonopolization and competition are needed at every level of the food production, distribution, and marketing system if private agriculture is to succeed.

Creation of credit cooperatives, for example, should be one of the first steps in the development of the cooperative system. Lack of credit is a major obstacle for collective farmers who want to start their own farms.

In developing the cooperative movement, we should observe the following principles, learning from the experience of cooperatives around the world:

1. Establishing loan, credit, and saving cooperatives is an essential first step;

2. Supply-oriented cooperatives are better suited to changing economic conditions than marketing cooperatives;

3. Most farmer cooperatives should be multipurpose to increase their effectiveness;

4. The type of cooperative determines their management structure; for example, milk marketing cooperatives should be locally or regionally managed;

5. The success of cooperatives is largely determined by the experience and qualification of its members and managers;

6. Cooperatives can and should develop simultaneously throughout the food production, distribution, marketing, and farm supply systems to their mutual benefit;

7. The success of cooperatives depends on the implementation of supportive cooperative and agrarian policies.

The United States Can Help Develop Soviet Cooperatives

The United States should aid true cooperatives not pseudo-cooperatives, such as the consumer cooperatives and collective farms, which are linked to the old command economy. Some American firms are mistakenly supporting these collective farms and consumer cooperatives, which have generally opposed market reforms.

These "cooperatives" do have money, political clout, and the infrastructure to support and pay for Western programs. They do have central administrations, which makes program development easier. But these old institutions are not truly interested in change.

The United States should be supporting new, forward-thinking organizations, such as the Union of Amalgamated Cooperatives, not old-guard organizations, like the International Cooperative Alliance or Centrosoyuz.

The days of one-stop shopping when the West could work directly with a central ministry or organization are gone. Real help must be provided directly to republican, regional, and local private farmers' organizations. These programs — education, research, training, and technical assistance, agribusiness exchange programs, loans, grants, equity investments, and joint ventures — are vital in helping the Soviet Union move to a market economy.

7

Family Farming in the Soviet Union

G.I. Shmelev

T he Soviet Union compared with other former socialist countries tries has until recently had the most economically inefficient system of agricultural production and land distribution. The socioeconomic structure of the agricultural sector must now be substantially reformed. To accomplish this, radical changes must be made in the system of land use, ownership, and distribution.

The Soviet Union has the highest percentage of government-owned agricultural land and the lowest percentage of privately-owned land. In eastern Germany (the former GDR), Hungary, Poland, Romania, Yugoslavia, Czechoslovakia, as well as in Asian countries such as Mongolia, China, and Vietnam, government-owned farms account for only 8 to 30 percent of all agricultural land. In the Soviet Union, government-owned farms account for 68 percent of the land. In Bulgaria, Hungary, Romania, and eastern Germany, the private sector controls 10 to 14 percent of the land. The private sector in Yugoslavia and Poland controls 68 percent and 77 percent, respectively. This compares with 1.5 percent in the Soviet Union. These figures reflect the nationalization of land following the October Revolution and the resulting state and collective farm monopolies. Unfortunately, the experience of the Soviet Union and foreign countries shows that the private sector is much more efficient than the government-owned sector.

Family or individually-controlled agricultural production takes place primarily on household garden plots (*lichnie podsobniye khozyaistva*). In the Soviet Union, household plots are the traditional and most widespread form of individual agricultural production. They are considered part of the agroindustrial complex. Their primary reason for existence is to supplement a family's income and food supply. Since privatizing state and collective farms and the whole agroindustrial complex will take a long time, the family plot will remain the primary form of private agricultural production for some time. During the reform period, expansion and specialization of plots can be a natural and resource-efficient means of creating new peasant farms. The plot can be turned into a peasant farm when the plot holder stops working on the farm or non-farm enterprise and becomes the independent owner of the peasant farm.

Plots differ from peasant farms not only in their smaller size, but also because they help supplement incomes from an individual's primary work on a state or collective farm or some other enterprise. Plots are much smaller than the new peasant farms in the Soviet Union. Plots belonging to collective farm workers average only 0.3 hectares. Plots belonging to state farm workers are only about half that. Peasant farms, on the other hand, average about 31 hectares in size. The average size of a peasant farm in the Russian republic is 41 hectares. Plots have a total area of 9.5 million hectares, of which 8.8 million acres are used for agricultural production. Only 2.2 million hectares of land belong to peasant farms.

Plot Sizes Vary Republic to Republic

Sizes of plots belonging to collective farm workers vary widely by republic. In Lithuania, for example, plots are on the average more than 0.5 hectare in size, while plots in Turkmenia, Kazakhstan, and Tajikistan are only about .08 to .09 hectare. On the average, 100 plots support 128 head of cattle, including 73 milking cows. In addition, 100 plots support 88 pigs, 129 head of sheep and goats, 1,150 head of poultry, and 16 beehives.

It is impossible to draw a strict line between a plot and a peasant farm. There are several important steps necessary to expand a plot into a peasant farm. First, the size of land in use must be expanded to the legal maximum set for plots. Then the primary members of the family must quit their jobs as state farm or enterprise workers. Finally, the farm must become a legal entity and begin to produce goods primarily intended for sale off the farm. Plots are important not only because they produce one-fourth of the country's gross agricultural product, but also because they are the basis for the formation of peasant farms.

Comparisons of yield rates show that plots are relatively efficient, with their yields often greatly surpassing public sector yields. However, yields for vegetables not grown in greenhouses are only 2 centners per hectare higher on plots than on state and collective farms.

The following table compares yields for public and private sector production in 1990. (yields in centners per hectare)

Crop	State/collective farm yields	Private sector yields	percent difference
Grain (excl. corn)	19.5	26.7	37
Oil-bearing crops (mostly sunflowers)	12.8	22.5	76
Potatoes	95.8	117.4	22
Melons (for human consumption)	67.9	159.0	234
Melons (for feed)	88.7	200.6	226
Annual grass hay	17.8	44.4	249
Perennial grass hay	26.3	53.8	204
Fruits & berries (Total)	36.6	46.4	27
Berries	16.9	45.6	270
Grapes	57	114.6	201
Nuts	2.1	11.3	538
Citrus fruits	56.5	264.6	468

Since 1990, data have been collected on peasant farm yields, permitting comparisons with state and collective farm yields. Yield rates for a number of primary crops grown on peasant farms exceed yield rates not only on state and collective farms, but also on plots. In 1990, the yield for potatoes on peasant farms was 146.9 centners per hectare, 53 percent higher than centners/hectare produced on state and collective farms yields, and 25 percent higher than plot yields. Likewise, the yield for forage root crops was 416.7 centners per hectare on peasant farms, which is 30 percent higher than on state and collective farms, and over 169 percent higher than the 154.4 centners/hectare produced on plots. The yield for vegetables on peasant farms was 179.2 centners/hectare, 16 percent above the centners/hectare on state and collective farms and 14.7 percent above the relative plot yield.

For livestock, fertility is higher in the private sector than in the government-owned sector. In 1990, for every 100 females, 80 calves were born in the government-owned sector while 85 calves were born in the private sector. For 100 females, the government sector produced 1,194 piglets, and 88 lambs and goat kids, while the private sector produced 1,225 piglets and 98 lambs and goat kids. The average slaughterweight of pigs, sheep, and goats in the private sector is higher than in the public sector. Thirty-four percent more honey is extracted from a plot beehive than a beehive on a state or collective farm.

The private sector produces the overwhelming portion of high-value products. In 1990, for example, the private sector produced 95 percent of all rabbit meat and 71 percent of all honey. The majority of silkworm cocoons, which produce raw material for silk, can be found in the private sector. The private sector produces 53 percent of all fruits and berries, including 82 percent of citrus fruits, 86 percent of berries, and 92.5 percent of nuts. It also produces 65 percent of the country's potatoes.

The importance of the private sector for the food supply of the country has grown substantially in light of the refusal of many state and collective farms to engage in small-scale dairy production. In 1988, six percent of Soviet state and collective farms did not have any large cattle. In Georgia, Azerbaijan, Kirgizia, Tajikistan, Armenia, and Turkmenia these figures are from 15 to 23 percent. Thirty-three percent of state and collective farms didn't have pigs.

In Uzbekistan, Kazakhstan, Azerbaijan, Kirgizia, and Tajikistan 70 to 90 percent of the state and collective farms didn't have any pigs. Sixty percent of state and collective farms didn't have any sheep or goats. Seventy percent of state and collective farms didn't have any poultry.

In the non-black earth zone of the RSFSR, and in Byelorussia, Kazakhstan, Georgia, Lithuania, Armenia, and Estonia, no poultry was found on 90 to 94 percent of state and collective farms. Obviously, in regions where state and collective farms don't produce these forms of meat, milk, or poultry products, rural family tables and grocery stores can get these products only from peasant yards.

Certain changes are taking place in the structure of the means of production on plots. Because of a lack of mechanization, an increase in the size of plots, and growth in the number of peasant farms, the number of horses in the private sector has grown considerably. In 1980 there were around 572,000 horses in the private sector, and by 1990 the number was over one million. The private sector owned 20 percent of these horses. The private sector also owns the majority of donkeys and mules, which are widely used in the Central Asian republics and in the Caucasus.

In 1990, 1.7 percent of the total fixed productive capital in agriculture was located in plots. If cattle are included, this percentage increases to 5.3 percent. At the beginning of 1990 the total fixed productive capital of plots was 6.2 billion rubles (without cattle). Considering that state and collective farms have a relatively high level of mechanization compared to the private sector, one could assume that human labor on government farms has a high level of productivity (as defined by the value of output produced by an individual). That, however, is not the case. In 1990, according to the data collected, collective farm families performed almost 30 percent of their labor on plots. In the same year, however, plots produced 24 percent of the gross agricultural output of the country. That figure highlights the extremely low productivity of labor on state and collective farms. More than 95 percent of the labor on state and collective farms is performed by men and women of working age, while only 80 percent of the labor on plots is performed by people of working age. In fact, a large portion of labor on plots is performed by retirees and children. Also, harsher working conditions on plots influence the vitality of the labor. Most work on state and collective farms happens during the first half of the day. Plot work comes after when the workers are tired and less efficient.

Plots Produce Higher Quality Goods

In comparing production efficiency, it is also interesting to look at the better shelf-life of privately-grown produce. In the government-owned sector, losses range from 25 to 35 percent of the total harvest. The better quality of privately grown produce is readily apparent when comparing the shelves of state grocery stores with farm-market benches.

Of course, it's important to remember that there are many regions of the country (mountainous regions of the northern Caucasus, the Carpathians, etc.) where it is impossible, at least without specialized equipment, to work the soil and sow with machinery. Where natural conditions do not permit large-scale production, the economic effectiveness of small-scale family production is much greater.

Finally, when comparing the economic effectiveness of small-scale and large-scale production, it is important to remember that this discussion is not about small-scale farming, such as one finds in Europe, but about extremely small-scale farming. The relative productivity of plots indicates not so much the high efficiency of the plots themselves, but the very low efficiency of the large-scale, centrally controlled state and collective farms.

Data on the economic efficiency of various types of production in Eastern Europe lead to the same conclusions. These data indicate a better use of material and energy resources on family plots compared to government-run farms. The ratio of agricultural production to fixed productive capital is 1.5 to 2 times higher for family farm operations than for the state and cooperative sectors. A low level of capital and material consumption is a unique feature of family farms. In Hungary in 1988, for example, small private farms produced 38 percent of the gross agricultural output and 57 percent of the net output. Statistics in Hungary indicate that in 1988 private farms produced 75 kilograms of meat per capita compared to 17.5 kilograms per capita in the USSR. In Hungary, private farms produced 287 eggs per capita, while the private sector produced only 75 in the USSR. Of course, the private sector in Hungary controls 13 percent of the land, while in the Soviet Union it only controls 1.5 percent. Also, the government-owned sector in Hungary actively cooperates with small individual farms, especially in supplying feed.

Another particular feature of plots is their ability, under favorable conditions, to increase their level of productivity in a short time. In Hungary, for example, the production of pork in the private sector increased 12.5 times from 1970 to 1984. The private sector's portion of the total output of pork rose from 11 percent to 47 percent during that period. In Vietnam, support for livestock husbandry on private plots and peasant farms led to a 240 percent increase in the number of cattle and sheep in the private sector from 1980 to 1987.

Right now, the importance of plots is growing. The following factors explain this growth:

1. The agrarian crisis in the USSR and increasingly severe food supply problems have increased the importance of their production.

2. Plots have a significant potential for growth, particularly in fruit and vegetable production and livestock raising.

3. Economic growth requires tremendous capital investment, which is severely limited. Plots can be an important way of conserving capital investment. The experience of the Soviet Union and other countries shows that plots are much more efficient in their use of capital investments in comparison to state and collective farms. Plots can, under favorable conditions, quickly increase their volume of production in a short period of time.

4. Unfavorable demographic conditions in the agricultural sector create a situation where there are now around 10 million collective farm retirees, whose labor can only be utilized through plots.

It is worth paying some attention to the rapid growth of peasant farms in the Soviet Union. Although peasant farms first began to appear only in 1987, they are now more than 70,000 (not including the peasant farms of Armenia). There are 32,000 peasant farms in Russia and about 15,000 in the Baltics. Peasant farms are also growing in Georgia. In 1989, the Council of Ministers issued a decree calling for the priority development of peasant farms to replace economically unsuccessful collective and state farms in six regions. By March 1991, there were 21,000 peasant farms in Georgia. Georgia recently decided to organize peasant farms in another 25 mountainous regions of the republic. The creation of peasant farms in Armenia is taking place very quickly. In Armenia, 566 collective farms have been liquidated and transformed into more than 150,000 individual farms and

18,000 collective peasant farms which cover a territory of 300,000 hectares.

By contrast, in many large republics, particularly the Ukraine and Byelorussia, there are very few private farms. There are also few private farms in the Central Asian republics. In January 1991 peasant farms had only 0.7 million hectares of land. By June 1991, 2.2 million hectares of land belonged to peasant farms.

The role that peasant farms will play in the socioeconomic structure of agriculture will depend largely on well they are supplied with material and technical inputs, on the establishment of a market relations, and on competition in the agrarian economy. Competition is beginning to play a large role in the entire structure of the agroindustrial complex.

Because rural inhabitants in many regions are uncertain about the stability of agrarian policies, there is a limited number of people who are willing to create peasant farms. This number is also limited by negative relations between peasant farmers and the leadership and workers of state and collective farms. There are frequent cases of collective farm workers denouncing private farmers as "kulaks," destroying peasant crops, and forcing peasants, especially new settlers, to leave their farms. These conditions explain the "wait-and-see" attitude of those who, under more favorable conditions and better relations, would set up their own farms.

Many New Farmers Are City People

Who are the people who own peasant farms? In many unpopulated regions of Russia, farmers are settlers from cities. Nonetheless, many of those settlers originally came from villages or had parents or grandparents who were peasants. Some new farmers are settlers from other parts of the country. These new settlers can't create their farms by expanding plots. They must create peasant farms, which is more difficult since they often have little knowledge of local conditions.

At the present stage of development, private farmers are highly dependent on collective farms, state farms, and other public sector enterprises and organizations. Peasant farmers must buy young animals, silage, feed concentrates, hay, and machinery from these farms. Many peasant farmers must lease buildings from state and collective farms. In 1990, state and collective farms supplied 30 to 40 percent of the fertilizer and fuel needed by leaseholders, peasant farms, and new agricultural cooperatives. State and collective farms supplied one-fourth of the tractors. Approximately two-thirds of fertilizers, tractors, and trucks on private farms came from Gosagroprom enterprises. In some republics, especially in Byelorussia, from half to two-thirds of fuel, fertilizer, and equipment (tractors, combines, and cars) came from state and collective farms. Because state and collective farms and agricultural machinery producers have monopoly ownership of the means of production, they can enslave private farmers, who have no alternative sources, as unequal partners in agreements. Moreover, state and collective farms are unreliable partners for farmers, often violating or hindering the fulfillment of agreements.

Private farms in existence for more than a year want to reduce their dependence on state and collective farms. They can do this by increasing the amount of land used to produce feed, by making direct agreements with procurement or processing enterprises (thus bypassing state and collective farms), and by buying, instead of leasing, their equipment.

Peasant farms are still poorly supplied. According to state figures, more than 80 percent of the peasant farmers polled in 1990 reported insufficient material and equipment supplies. Many complained of a low level of mechanization and that the agricultural machinery was too expensive and of poor quality. Peasant farms are particularly poorly supplied with equipment. Things are a little better for plot holders in terms of small machinery. In 1990, 2,200 mini-tractors were produced, as well as 126,000 motorized cultivators, and 45,000 trailers. As a rule, enterprises producing small equipment and garden implements are not specialized, but rather produce them as a sideline or secondary product. Many types of equipment needed for farms are not produced at all. If the availability of equipment doesn't improve soon, there may be a decline in the formation of new farms and an increase in failures of existing farms.

In this connection, converted defense industry factories can play an important role in producing equipment for peasant farms and plots. Acquisition of used equipment from abroad can also play an important role. In addition, there is also a place for international cooperation in the joint production of specialized, small-scale equipment for family farms and plots. Cooperatives could also produce essential equipment. At the same time, it is essential to create commercial centers for the sale, leasing, and repair of small equipment for peasant farms.

Owners of peasant farms and plots have high hopes that new organizations, such as the Association of Peasant Farms and Agricultural Cooperatives of Russia (AKKOR), the Association of Plot Owners of Uzbekistan, can represent their interests. Government programs work through these extremely vital organizations to help farmers. However, there is a danger that these organization will themselves become a part of the bureaucratic structure.

The RSFSR Council of Ministers has recently adopted a series of laws and decrees designed to aid the development of peasant farms. These include the decree "On Supporting the Development of Peasant Farms, Related Associations, Unions, and Cooperatives" adopted in January 1991 and the decree "On Supplementary Measures for Developing Peasant Farms and Agricultural Cooperatives in the Russian Republic" adopted in June 1991.

At this early stage in the formation and strengthening of peasant farms, it is important to adopt policies that stimulate the private sector and ensure its place in the structure of the Soviet agricultural economy. The peasant farm, given proper conditions, has the potential to become a highly productive and economically efficient agricultural enterprise. Although plots can fulfill a certain consumer demand, they have poor prospects for playing a large role in the market. In the short term, however, plots will play an extremely important role and cannot be fairly compared to peasant farms.

8

Development of Rural Life
And Agriculture in Estonia: 1992-94

Ivar Raig

The Estonian government has three goals in its drive to eliminate the negative effects of Soviet domination and reemerge as a thriving market economy. The main features of this program, initiated during 1991, are institution- and infrastructure-building, comprehensive privatization, and commercialization of agriculture and industry. The program's goals are to:

1. Satisfy local needs from domestic production.

2. Ensure basic economic security by exporting enough products to the former Soviet Union to guarantee adequate energy and supplies of essential raw materials.

3. Establish and expand hard-currency export markets in the West. These markets would potentially free Estonia from dependence on the former Soviet republics for essential resources.

Given its historic importance in Estonia's economy, a revitalized food sector and sustained, food-product export campaign are pivotal elements in the success of Estonia's program.

Four thousand smaller farms have already been privatized, but over 300, inefficient, and very large state and collective farms — mostly dairy and beef farms that average 4,150 hectares — await privatization and commercialization.

Sustained domestic economic vitality and hard-currency export earnings require a modern, efficient, profit-seeking food products network capable of transforming raw farm products into salable, value-added products. Like the Scandinavian economies, successful export promotion and export-led growth are especially vital to Estonia's drive to regain the economic vitality of its pre-Soviet period.

During the Soviet period, Estonia exported 30 to 40 percent of its food to the Soviet Union in exchange for fuel, feed grains, pesticides, and fertilizer. Soviet-Estonian trade has fallen dramatically since August, and Estonia has lost both its main source of imports and outlet for products. Food output fell 15 percent in 1991, after declining 10 percent in 1990.

The key to reversing the food sector's decline, unless the old trading patterns can be quickly reestablished, will be lowering dependence on foreign fuel, grain, fertilizer, pesticides, and machinery; greatly increasing farm-to-market efficiency; diversifying the dairy and beef farms; and penetrating new export markets.

Rural life in Estonia will be fundamentally affected as the major land ownership and enterprise reform process begins taking effect in 1992. Policy makers must be guided by several fundamental principles during this extremely difficult period:

1. Moving from a command economy, where all resources were state owned, to private ownership of land and means of production requires a fundamental relearning process for all ages and social groups.

2. Domestic prices must move toward world-market levels if Estonia is to develop an internationally competitive food sector.

3. Reforms must work within current divisions of labor, product specialization, and Estonia's comparative advantages in world markets.

4. Government subsidies and grants to farmers must be minimized, since they increase industry's tax burdens without stimulating agricultural efficiency.

5. Diversified rural development will be helped if a wide range of businesses locate in rural Estonia.

Population Is 30 Percent Rural

Estonia's rural population was 446,833, or 28.4 percent of the country's total population, in 1989, compared to 447,650 and 30.3 percent, respectively, in 1979. The rural population grew by 2,200 persons in 1990, but remained 30.3 percent of the total population, according to national census figures.

The ethnic composition of Estonia's rural population has not changed in the 10 years. It remains 87.5 percent Estonian, 8.5 percent Russian, 1.3 percent Ukrainian, 1.2 percent Finn, 0.5 percent Byelorussian, and 1 percent other nationalities.

Males make up 46.8 percent of the rural population. Fifty-six percent are of working age, 26 percent are younger, and 12 percent are beyond working age. The share of working-age males in the past 20 years has increased and that of older men has decreased.

Females make up 53.2 percent of Estonia's rural population. Forty-eight percent of rural females are of working age; 26 percent are younger; and 32 percent are beyond working age.

The education level of the rural population is lower than in towns where most cultural, educational, and scientific institutions are located. Still, the level of rural education is satisfactory.

General Features of the Agricultural Sector

Estonian agriculture has developed within the constraints of centralized planning during the Soviet period. Crop yields have changed little during the past 15 years, but resource consumption has increased dramatically, reflecting the central authorities' focus on production rather than efficient resource utilization.

State purchasing and pricing policy has been arbitrary and has excluded the cost of fodder and the value of protein. Its forced reorganization of Estonian agriculture toward greater emphasis on beef and swine production neglected the dairy industry's traditional role as the most significant source of protein in the Estonian diet.

The claimed advantages of large-scale collective and state farms in using machinery and buildings efficiently never materialized. Instead, poor management led to increased farm losses, transportation costs, and to soil, groundwater, and environmental degradation.

Because of the departmentalized character of the system of state orders during the Soviet period, Estonian agriculture and industry have been divorced from one another. This isolation of agriculture, combined with production quotas rather than profit potential as a motivator for business activity, has made Estonian agriculture almost totally dependent on imported resources, about 90 percent of which came from the Soviet Union.

Independence, plus the collapse of the Soviet distribution and trading system, caused significant declines in imports of fodder grain, fuel, metals, and machinery from the Soviet Union in 1991. It is likely that these imports will decrease even more as Estonia must now pay for them at world-market prices and in convertible currency.

According to recent estimates, 1990 Estonian imports from the Soviet Union, valued at world prices and excluding concentrated fodder, totaled approximately U.S. $1 billion. Imports from third countries were at least U.S. $100 million. Estonian commodity exports, by contrast, totalled only U.S. $450 to 550 million, plus timber exports of U.S. $30 million. This almost two-to-one import/export ratio can probably not be changed quickly. Thus there is a great need to concentrate on methods of making agriculture more efficient and reducing imports.

Because of the political changes and economic crisis in the former Soviet Union, the command economic system is no longer functioning in Estonian agriculture. There is utter confusion and decay on the collective farms. Cattle are being sold and slaughtered to cover current expenses. As they attempt to reorganize, state farms can no longer get resources from the Soviet Union. New private family farms face shortages and high prices and will be unable to provide a stable food supply in the near future.

To make matters worse in the short term, restoration of family farms, confiscated by the government in 1940, is depriving large-scale, cattle-breeding enterprises of their pastures and croplands. Therefore, until new private farms begin operating, Estonia is faced with a growing problem of unused, large farm buildings and production capacity.

Moreover, in moving toward a market economy, Estonia has abolished meat and milk subsidies, decreased the centralized allotment of resources, and has introduced virtually free domestic trade. In short, the state no longer controls private farmers as it did collective and state farms. But these new freedoms have not yet produced the necessary gains in agricultural efficiency.

Estonian agriculture must become twice as efficient to be competitive in Western Europe. Introducing private property and privately managed farms will stimulate management, moderate price rises, and stop the decline of production and depletion of wealth. Unfortunately, the lack of property laws is hampering the revitalization of the food sector.

Efforts to Privatize and Commercialize Estonian Farms

Privatization legislation enacted since 1989 makes specific provisions for returning Estonia's food sector to private hands:

1. Rehabilitation of ownership rights and returning property to or compensating former owners who can prove they held title prior to 1940.

2. Privatization of the property of collective and state farms by means of compensation and shares.

3. Transition to private enterprise, entrepreneurship, and the private ownership of businesses.

4. Transfer of administration of schools and social institutions to local municipalities.

5. Implementation of tax and budget reforms.

6. Formation of democratic-political structures.

The first stage of agrarian reform started with the adoption of the Farm Act by the Estonian SSR Supreme Soviet in November 1989. By the beginning of 1990, the first 1,000 family farms were registered in Estonia. By the beginning of 1991, the number of farms had grown to 4,000, and as of August 31, 1991, another 2,500 family farms were registered in Estonia. These farms had a total of 169,000 hectares of land, or an average of 26 hectares per farm. Unfortunately, only an estimated 72,800 hectares of this land can be cultivated (11.2 hectares per farm). Although these small family farms play an important role, they are not as competitive and efficient as larger farms and cannot support a household.

The second and the main stage of the agrarian reform will begin in early 1992, after all former farm and land owners have been registered and the Land Reform Act has been passed by the Supreme Court of the Republic of Estonia. Former owners of collectivized property and their inheritors, proceeding from the continuity of the right of inheritance, as well as producers of agricultural products, will be offered land and existing buildings free. Where it is impossible to restore land to its former owner, the former owner will be offered other land or compensated. In cases where farms were consolidated into much larger state farms, former owners will be given comparable land for family farms. The government will support the use of existing property and encourage its development by offering financing at very favorable rates.

Property, which remains unclaimed after the initial reclamation round is completed in spring 1992, will then be offered for sale. Money raised from these privatization sales will accrue to local governments and be used for development projects in local districts.

The Role of the State in Agricultural Development

During the transition to a market economy, the state will also help reorganize Estonian industry in order to reduce the dependence of Estonian agriculture on machinery and resources imported from the Soviet Union. The role of the state during the transition period includes:

1. Ensuring staple foodstuffs for the population.

2. Ensuring state purchases of agricultural produce necessary for commodity exchange.

3. Providing work and livelihood for the rural population.

4. Creating regulations to ensure the preservation of the environment.

5. Preserving and improving land as a national resource, taking into

consideration the prospective growth of world population, changes in the food market, and the decrease of cultivable land.

6. Guaranteeing the essential needs of the population in the case of natural, political, or social catastrophes.

As land is the greatest source of wealth in Estonia, it should command high prices. Products grown on the land will also eventually generate significant income taxes. In the near term, however, encouraging agricultural development will require a combination of low income taxes and temporary government subsidies. The government must also provide a social safety net and training programs for rural people who lose their jobs during reforms. The assistance of foreign countries will be helpful here.

During the transition period, agriculture will be subsidized by government credits. Credits will also be extended to industries that supply agriculture. The state will cover expenses for agricultural education, science, retraining, and a farm extension service. The state will also support the development of family farms and new enterprises with tax allowances.

Land taxes will be based on land quality and location. The market value of the land (at least 80 percent of the land rent) will serve as the basis for the property tax. Land which cannot be profitably used now will not be subject to property taxes, so long as it is used for agricultural purposes. Moreover, the government will subsidize marginal land to keep it in agricultural circulation.

The new structure of agricultural administration remains in a formative stage. The Ministry of Agriculture and agricultural departments continue to develop a central plan and allocate resources. A new, decentralized structure will require implementation of land reform and free-market prices. To that end, the tasks of the Ministry of Agriculture should include:

1. Directing scientific research.

2. Helping to establish an American-style farm extension service.

3. Introducing innovations through training programs or consultants.

4. Coordinating export and import of agricultural produce.

The existing system of agricultural education will be retained in the transition period. New higher educational institutions will be founded to expand and guarantee the availability of higher education. Scientists should be sent to foreign universities and research institutions for advanced training.

The government should fund agricultural education, advanced training, fundamental research, and the bulk of applied research. In addition, the government should fund plant and animal breeding and subsidize the production of veterinary medicine, pesticides, and the development of new technologies. The government should also establish a research center to analyze the export potential of Estonian agriculture and to promote agricultural efficiency.

The quality of Estonian rural life varies widely. In some areas, the presence of many collective or state farm has caused the local area to become quite urbanized. Other rural areas are almost empty and sparsely populated. The government, working through regional and local organizations, should fund social programs in underdeveloped areas. In addition, the government should attempt to diversify the rural economy after strengthening the agricultural sector and ensuring a stable food supply.

Estonia's rural life is extremely dependent now on agriculture. The main challenge in the near future is to retain the present level of agricultural production and to provide the population with ample foodstuffs. But in the course of the reorganization of Estonia, other branches of the economy must also be developed in the countryside as well.

Agricultural Production Needs: 1992-94

Crop products should provide 60 to 65 percent (1,200 to 1,300 grams per day) of people's daily food needs. Consumption of potatoes and grain products is close to the recommended quantities, while consumption of food oil, vegetables, and fruits are about two-thirds recommended norms. Estonians consume about 10 percent more sugar than is recommended.

Table I provides data on the basic minimum annual production levels to meet basic nutritional requirements. Up to half of domestic grain consumption and all food oil, vegetable fat, and sugar have been imported. Two-thirds of vegetable and half of berry and fruit demand is satisfied by domestically grown produce. Following independence and the collapse of the Soviet trading system, Estonia's ability to satisfy these needs through imports has been severely curtailed.

Wheat and oats shares of total field crop production have been growing. Turnip rape (for producing food oil) cultivation will be increased 5,000 to 10,000 hectares by 1994. Total acreage under crop cultivation will be increased 5 percent, while that allocated to forage production (dry hay and haylage) will decrease 5 to 10 percent.

Table I
Minimum Production Levels, Selected Food Commodities
1992-94

Products	Per Capita Output (Kg)	Total Annual Output(1,000 ton)
Grains - flour	100	160
Grain		250
Potatoes	110	175
Vegetables	120	190
Fruits and berries	80	120
Food oil	14	22
Sugar	39	69

It is not possible or economically justifiable in the near future to expand the cultivation of sugar beets to meet Estonia's need for sugar. However, increasing the production of syrup from starch by 15,000 tons (from 5,000 tons to 20,000 tons) would substitute for 13,000 tons of imported beet sugar.

If fuel and fertilizer supplies do not decrease considerably, the per hectare yield of grains should be 2,100 to 2,200 kg, potatoes 15,000 to 16,000 kg, and grass feeds 2,800 food units between 1992 and 1994. Under the best case forecast, total feed crop yields are expected to decline 40 percent, or to 1,100 food units per hectare, by 1994.

In the event of crisis caused by severe fuel and fertilizer shortages, the grain acreage will most likely decline by 10,000 to 15,000 hectares, and the yield will most likely fall 40 percent to 800 to 900 kg per hectare. Three-fourths of the expected 50 percent decrease in hay yields per hectare will result from the lack of imported ammonium saltpeter and fewer mowings per season. Fuel shortages will also mean less acreage planted in feed vegetable and cabbage.

Berry, fruit, potato, and vegetable production for human consumption will not be as severely affected by the crisis, as the reduction in the acreage under crop in large-scale production will be compensated by the increase in family and other small-scale farms.

In the Estonian Rural Center Party's view, the following measures are necessary to increase crop production:

1. Seed cultivation, plant breeding, and cultivation of technical crops should be subsidized from the government budget.

2. Pesticides should be imported at an estimated cost of $20 million.

3. Estonia's fertilizer industry should start the production of complex

fertilizers.

4. A restructured Estonian industry should produce in a timely fashion appropriate agricultural machinery, spare parts, and efficient, energy-saving machinery and facilities, such as drying rooms to reduce losses of grains.

5. The restructuring of the Estonian economy should include creating a domestic, agricultural machinery and spare-parts industry, including:

a. Introduction of energy-saving technologies, like precision-seeding machines that can simultaneously apply fertilizers and seed, saving 15 to 20 percent in mineral fertilizers, and presses capable of keeping grains moist, at a 50 percent energy saving.

b. Construction of new grain drying and storage facilities to reduce losses and repair of existing ones.

c. Creation of potato storage and processing businesses and companies producing diversified value-added potato products (purees, dry products, starch, spirits) to increase both domestic consumption and exports.

6. Complete the construction of a major margarine factory which will create an increased demand for turnip rape seed and justify cultivation of an additional 10,000 to 30,000 hectares.

7. Total yield of grains can be increased by 100,000 tons by plowing an additional 100,000 hectares of low-valued land. Fifty thousand hectares can be put successfully into grains.

8. Increasing the acreage under legume (clover, alfalfa, trefoil, etc.) cultivation will significantly reduce nitrate fertilizer needs and contribute to meeting farm animals' protein requirements without importing high-protein concentrates.

Machinery and energy can best be used to raise grains, turnip rape seed, and grass plants. Potatoes, vegetables, and flax should be raised in farms and other small-scale production forms.

According to recommended consumption norms, Estonia must produce the following minimum quantities of basic animal products.

Table 2
Annual Dairy and Meat Production Requirements

Products	Per capita Production (Kg)	Total Production (1,000 tons)
Milk and dairy products	447	703
Meat and meat products	73-95	115-150

In order to buy 500,000 tons of cereals from the Soviet Union under the same conditions as in 1991, we will have to sell 30,000 tons of meat and 350,000 tons of milk. In that case we can meet recommended norms for the Estonian people and have nearly 150,000 tons of milk left over.

If we cannot import feed grain, we can still meet our own dairy products needs. But we can only produce and sell to our people 75,000 to 80,000 tons of meat (in slaughterweight), which is approximately 60 percent of recommended needs.

In the current crisis, livestock production has drastically declined, and people are able to acquire only 25 percent of their meat needs and 66 percent of their milk and dairy products needs. The population of young stock, fatting bulls, and pigs will continue to decrease until 1994-95, mainly because of the shortage of appropriate feed. The population of cows will also decrease due to the intensive program to control and eradicate leukosis from Estonia's cow herd. The availability of food will be reduced further by disruptions caused by the breakdown of the centralized supply of spare parts and refrigeration equipment. Without these problems, there is adequate processing capacity to meet demand.

A major contention of the Estonian Rural Center Party is that state support, amounting to at least 50 percent of expenditures on animal breeding in family farms, is absolutely necessary to guarantee the continuity of animal breeding. In order to avoid major depletions of current breeding stock, the central government, through the Ministry of Agriculture, must import medicines and diagnostic equipment from the West and strive to promote their production in Estonia.

These problems are compounded by the outdated and dysfunctional condition of agricultural buildings (dairy, swine, and poultry barns) and equipment. Huge concrete barns, characteristic of Soviet agriculture, have no place in a system of small, private farms. Revitalizing Estonia's agriculture will require designing new facilities and using local materials, such as the region's abundant timber.

Foreign Energy Consumption Must Be Reduced

Prior to independence and the breakup of the Soviet Union, Estonian agriculture and rural life functioned mainly on imported fuel. Domestic fuels and electric heating met only 10 to 12 percent of local requirements. Following independence, the government's stated goal is to achieve dramatic reductions in dependence upon foreign energy sources through a program of increased reliance on domestic fuels (timber, pressed peat, oil shale, and shale oil), and by increasing the share of cheaper imported fuels (coal and gas).

Current oil and gas requirements, presented in Table 3, are forecast to decline by U.S. $60 million, or 27 percent under current energy-saving plans. These reductions will allow the economy to operate at current levels, but only if convertible currency shortages do not curtail energy supplies further, thereby precipitating a crisis.

Low-capacity boilers and auxiliary equipment will be installed, and if a crisis develops, energy-intensive production, such as greenhouses and grain driers, will be suspended. Decentralized heating of houses in settlements will be initiated with the installation of solid fuel boilers in individual cellars. Local production of the necessary equipment is beginning.

Table 3
Estonian Fuel Requirements

Fuel	Consumption (1,000 tons)	Price U.S.$/ton	Cost Million U.S.$
Black Oil	386.0	93.2	36.0
Gas (mil. in^3)	187.2	73.6	13.8
Coal	100.5	39.6	4.0
Kerosene	63.4	192.6	12.2
Petrol	178.0	442.3	78.7
Diesel oil	224.0	345.1	77.3
Total			222.0

Forecasts for electric energy requirements reflect the expectation that local fuel production will expand and recognize the difficulties in finding substitutes for electric motors and electrical equipment. Whether electricity demand remains the same or falls depends on the use of intensive, electricity-consuming installations, such as greenhouses.

According to the Ministry of Agriculture, average annual electricity consumption in the agricultural sector has remained fairly constant over the past several years:

Table 4
Annual Electricity Requirements, Agricultural Sector

Category	Consumption (mill. KWH)
Machinery on collective and state farms	1,170
"Estonian Village Construction"	12
Grain Manufacturing	68
Total	1,358

The average price of electricity during the period was 6 kopecks/ KWH in the Soviet Union, and $.05/KWH in Western countries. Valued at Western prices, then, Estonia's farm sector consumes U.S.$68 million annually, with little prospect of any significant reductions in the foreseeable future.

Prior to independence, Estonia purchased most of its technical, agricultural equipment from the Soviet Union and East Germany. Two-thirds of this equipment does not meet world standards. Most of the feed is gathered with machines produced in the former German Democratic Republic. These machines will become useless if Estonia cannot buy spare parts.

With the development of new farms and the increased need for machines and equipment, Estonian hopes to produce agricultural machinery with the help of Western investment. Estonia already produces agricultural machines and components worth about 70 million rubles a year. Cooperative agreements with several foreign firms have been signed, but many problems, such as obtaining manufacturing inputs, remain.

Estonia recognizes the important role Western agribusiness can play in easing its transition toward a market-based agrarian system. The Estonian government has firmly signalled its pragmatic policy toward foreign investment through a variety of reform laws. The new legislation makes it possible, for instance, for foreign banks to open offices on the territory of Estonia.

Estonia has other advantages which make it attractive to agribusiness: a skilled labor force, well-developed infrastructure, and a large market. Estonia's strategic location and history make it an ideal center for East-West trade and business initiatives.

As Estonia looks to the future, it sees immense potential for sustained mutually beneficial ties with Western agribusiness. While the medium and long-term outlook for Estonian agriculture is bright, Estonia needs immediate, short-term humanitarian aid and farm credits to enable it to survive the winter and to pursue further reforms.

9

The Soviet Food Problem
and Land Reform

Barbara Severin

L and reform is frequently cited as the key to solving the low productivity and high cost of Soviet agricultural production and resolving the country's chronic food problem, that is, providing Soviet citizens with a diet that is roughly equivalent to those of other industrialized nations. Land reform, however, is only one of the many changes and reforms needed if the former USSR is to resolve these long-standing problems. Moreover, immediate breakup of state and collective farms in favor of small-scale, private farms, a course many Westerners and Soviet reformers advocate, can only lead to more chaos and disarray in the agriculture and food sector. The following paper addresses the dissatisfaction with food supplies and the reasons for it; outlines the role of private-sector agriculture in the former USSR and discusses prospects for peasant farms; and looks at the conditions under which Soviet agriculture and the food delivery system could begin to satisfy, the needs of Soviet consumers.

Growing Dissatisfaction

Since Mikhail Gorbachev took over the reins of government in 1985, the Soviet public's dissatisfaction with available food supplies has grown increasingly acute. The March 1989 plenum, which focused largely on the food problem and agrarian reform, delegated responsibility to the republics for managing day-to-day operation of the agricultural and food processing sectors as a way to improve local food supplies.[1] It also gave the right to

The views expressed in this text are my own and not necessarily those of the Central Intelligence Agency.

individuals to lease for a period of years small amounts of land to farm, formalizing a program that had been in an experimental stage for several years. The plenum, however, sidestepped several issues that continued to limit production and distribution of food. Little was done to change the state and collective farm structure or to break the bureaucratic stranglehold over Soviet farms, resolve the near impasse in food processing and distribution, better integrate the food supply system, or curtail the rapidly rising demand for food resulting from sharp growth in incomes while prices for most foods remained at fixed levels.

With the rise of nationalism in 1990, interrepublic trade of all goods and services began breaking down, and consumer dissatisfaction with food supplies increased even more rapidly than during the previous five years. Through 1991, republics attempted to increase their control over their own affairs and reduce or eliminate the center's authority. Increasing and improving local food supplies have been among the republics' greatest concerns. With winter approaching, agricultural output declining, and food shortages already widespread, the food-supply problem has an obvious near-term importance to republic leaders, eager to defend their newly-won political powers and fearful of a consumer backlash. According to numerous public opinion surveys, the availability and quality of food have long been perceived as the most important determinants of Soviet living standards.[2] While much of the old Soviet reality has changed enormously as a result of the revolutionary events since August 1991, the public's dissatisfaction with overall food supplies is certain to persist and to present a long-term challenge to authorities at all levels.

Until 1991, most Soviet consumers were less disturbed by the quantity of available food than by the poor quality, limited selection, and time needed to find and purchase food. This unsatisfactory state was the result of a food production and distribution system in which every major element — farms, transportation and storage, food processing, and wholesale and retail trade — was poorly equipped. In addition, Soviet agriculture suffered from a lack of economic incentives, excessive centralization, and no effective coordination.[3] Under Gorbachev, the problem was compounded by a rapid increase in money incomes, which when coupled with only limited increases in the availability of nonfood consumer goods, sharply stimulated demand for better quality food. The retail price increases of April 1, 1991, dampened growth in demand for food products somewhat according to Soviet press reports. However, the declining value of the ruble and consumer fears of still higher prices continue to empty shelves in state retail stores which sell well over half of all food.[4]

The very breadth of the food supply problem, its many causes, and the long neglect by the authorities of all aspects of food supply except for on-farm production argue that there is no single or simple solution such as breaking up state and collective farms, dramatically privatizing farm production through land reform, or allowing market forces to determine production. Resolving the food problem will be a difficult and lengthy process, and one that must be approached with some caution to avoid merely shifting current bottlenecks from one location to another. In addition, the role of government, be it central or republic or some combination, is likely to remain very important. In most of the world, the agro-food sector is an area of relatively extensive government intervention and support that is constantly affected by government policy. In particular, agricultural production is not directed by a truly "free market" in the traditional supply-and-demand sense of the word. Although farmers do have freedom to make their own decisions, and certainly have the freedom to fail, their decisions frequently are guided by official policy. Any doubts about the importance of government policy in influencing farm production, or of farmers' influencing government policy, are quickly laid to rest by a look at the General Agreement on Tariffs and Trade (GATT) discussions over the past several years.

Sources of the Food Problem

Contrary to the perception that farm production in the USSR is a disaster, official statistics indicate that the gross value of output grew at roughly twice the rate of population during the 1960-1990 period. That growth, however, was achieved at a very high cost financially and in terms of resources, particularly labor. The farm sector alone absorbed roughly 20 percent of investment resources (excluding housing and services) and of the labor force. State subsidies to cover the differences between relatively low stable retail food prices and procurement prices paid to farms grew enormously and by 1990 had risen well above 100 billion rubles, or over 20 percent of the state budget. The 1990 Plan called for paying out 116.5 billion rubles as subsidies.[5] Because of very large 1990 farm production, total subsidies probably exceeded the Plan's target. On-farm costs of production of most major farm products nearly doubled between 1970 and 1989, but yields increased by much smaller percentages.[6]

The blame for the unsatisfactory state of Soviet food supplies, however, also falls on each of the organizations traditionally involved in food production—farms, farm suppliers, procurement organizations, food-processing enterprises, and the trade network. Transportation and storage facilities on-farm and off are also woefully inadequate.[7] Until Gorbachev's advent, investment in food processing industries was woefully neglected; as a result, the industry is relatively primitive. Moreover, the lack of coordination among these organizations causes enormous losses — 30 to 50 percent of some products — as commodities move from farm to retail outlet, which substantially reduces the benefits of increased production.[8] At each stage of the chain, organizations were rewarded for meeting gross output targets. There were no substantial penalties for failing to supply enterprises at the next stage with high-quality inputs in a timely fashion. Finally, the traditional centralization of Soviet economic planning and management has hindered innovation and made coordination extremely difficult. Clearly, increasing farm production through land reform will not be sufficient to resolve the food problem. Why, then, does it seem to so many to be the solution?

Traditional Private-Sector Agriculture

Many Westerners regard Soviet private-sector agriculture as highly productive, noting that about 25 percent of the USSR's total value of production comes from three percent of the land.[9] This level of production, however, largely reflects the concentration of individuals and households on high-value, labor-intensive commodities such as livestock products, costlier vegetables (onions and cucumbers instead of cabbage) fruits, and herbs. To a lesser extent, it also stems from greater labor input — the use of pensioners, children, and so on — per unit of land. Greater labor input should increase yields, and, indeed, crude calculations suggest that yields of potatoes and other vegetables on plots are nearly 25 percent higher than on state and collective farms and yields of fruit about 70 percent higher. Output of milk per cow and eggs per chicken, however, is lower in the private sector, probably because of the difficulty of acquiring feedstuffs.[10] The private sector relies almost entirely on the socialized sector for the feed it needs to produce 26 percent of total meat, 21 percent of milk, and 26 percent of eggs.[11]

   Our calculations indicate that if all the land in the socialized sector that directly or indirectly produces feedstuffs for the private sector is added to official private plot holdings, the total land area required to support private plot production in 1987 was roughly 105 million hectares, or nearly 20 percent of all the arable land in the USSR. The relatively small amount of feedstuffs that individuals were able to purchase through the state system or from farms, and the several million tons of bread fed to livestock annually, technically result from labor input and the income thus earned. Misunderstanding the reasons for private-sector agricultural productivity appears to have fostered the idea that merely breaking up state and collective farms into millions of private farms would sharply increase agricultural productivity and thus resolve the food problem. Although some productivity gains could be achieved by moving toward private holding of land, owned or leased, the difficulties of moving product from producer to consumer and the enormous waste that occurs throughout the process suggest that gains to the consumer would be limited at best.

Except for private plots, there has been almost no private land in the former USSR since collectivization took place in the late 1920s and early 1930s. Gorbachev, however, recognized that long-term land leases, 10 to 15 years in length, could increase personal responsibility and raise productivity.[12] In 1985, he began making positive references to family farms and by early 1988 he was calling for the expansion of lease contracting in which individuals, groups, or families lease land and equipment from farms and contract to deliver specified farm products.[13] By 1989, land reform legislation was proposed, and in March 1990 all-union legislation was adopted. The legislation gave republics the right to determine how to proceed within their own boundaries.[14]

Land Reform

The legislation represented a relatively liberal view of land tenure but stopped short of endorsing private land ownership in the Western sense and did not authorize the purchase or sale of land.[15] It also granted key authority over land transfer to the lowest level of government — the local and regional "soviets" or councils. By mid-1991, 12 of the former 15 republics had initiated land reform laws and the process was underway. (Georgia, Uzbekistan, and Tajikistan have not yet published draft legislation although the topic is being discussed.) The laws differ considerably — a comparative analysis would be useful as the republics and Baltic countries strive to develop more independent economies. All republics and countries, however, include provision for peasant or farmer's farms. A peasant farmer has possession of his farm for life and can bequeath it to his heirs so long as it remains in agricultural use.

Implementation of the various laws varies widely, and the numerous, sometimes conflicting, statistical reports being released make evaluation tentative at best. There is general agreement, however, that during the period between July 1, 1990, and July 1, 1991, many republics made progress toward establishing peasant farms, at least in terms of numbers, which more than doubled to 70,000 farms covering about 4.5 million acres.[16] Although this represents only one percent of the total sown area, it does mark a beginning. Within the republics, the status appears to differ widely. Tajikistan, for example, reportedly has no peasant farms. By May 1991, Armenia, in contrast, had privatized 80 percent of its farm land.[17] How many of these farms in Armenia and elsewhere are producing agricultural commodities and how much they are producing is unclear. Anecdotal evidence suggests that yields on these farms, particularly of livestock products, are well above state and collective farm yields. At the same time, bureaucratic interference and the difficulties of beginning a new farm have hindered the progress of a substantial number and have forced other operators to give up their attempts. Moreover, if survey results are representative, no more than 10 to 20 percent of farm workers want to try independent farming.[18]

Near-Term Prospects

State and collective farms, together with interfarm enterprises and subsidiary farms established by industrial enterprises and military groups to ensure their own food supplies, produce about three-quarters of total agricultural output, and they will continue to do so for at least several years. Despite their acknowledged inefficiency and costliness, they have machinery, equipment, and a relatively knowledgeable labor force. Land reforms to date are a significant ideological breakthrough and have the potential to improve productivity. But achieving privatization on a broad scale will be a long, slow process.

Legislation, which provides a much-needed legal foundation for peasant farms, also gives existing state and collective farms the right to "permanent" possession. However, the legislation lacks a mechanism to ensure independent farmers access to good land and material supplies, and many republic laws specify a maximum farm size that in many areas would not be sufficient to establish a viable farm except in highly specific circumstances such as specialty crops for restaurant use. The permitted size ranges from 11 acres in Armenia to as much as 300 acres in parts of Russia. Several republics have specified no more than 110 acres. The average size of collective farms is roughly 15,000 acres and of state farms, roughly 38,000 acres.[19]

Despite the progress to date, the pace is glacially slow, and peasant farms still represent only a "drop in the bucket."[20] The disarray and turmoil surrounding the application process are daunting and the time involved more so.[21] The decades-long fear of entrepreneurship is still present, although some Western observers believe this is declining.[22]

Other serious impediments toward achieving an effective, relatively small-scale farming economy include:

• Lack of a structure to produce and deliver smaller scale inputs; only half of Russia's 29,000 private farmers has a tractor of any type.[23] Given the country's current balance-of-payments crisis, Western suppliers will not be willing to fill the gap on a large scale.

• Peasant farmers already complain about the difficulty of marketing output; many of them are unable to hire transportation, and rural procurement points refuse to buy their output or buy only at low prices.[24]

• The lack of roads and rural amenities including water and electricity in many parts of the country make establishing a peasant farm grueling work.

• The difficulties of financing private farming, particularly with the unsettled state of banks, the relative unfamiliarity of many Soviet farm workers with financial transactions, and relatively controlled prices seriously handicap private farm operation.[25]

Finally, and perhaps most important, is the basic question of whether peasant farming —owned or leased— is a viable way to a modern, efficient agricultural system that could provide an adequate diet for the entire country or for its constituent parts. Experience in the United States suggests it is not.

In the United States, there are many family farms owned by the operator. But few of these farms fit the Soviet peasant-farm model in terms of size or potential income generation. Fewer than 7 percent of U.S. farms are smaller than 110 acres, and those farms produce on average very low incomes, far from enough to support one person, to say nothing of a family. The average farm size in the United States in 1988 was about 460 acres; in that year, roughly 50 percent were larger than 1,200 acres and about half of those averaged about 2,600 acres, much smaller than state or collective farms in the former Soviet Union.[26]

The peasant-farm model in the USSR generally includes ownership — albeit under very restricted conditions — or long-term lease. However, Soviet law does not permit even a relatively free exchange of land. In the United States, only 35 percent of the land in farms is operated by full owners who are free to buy or sell as they wish, slightly more than half by part-owners, and the balance by tenants who seldom tie themselves to lengthy rental arrangements.[27] The Soviet model implies a family can earn an adequate income from its farm, presumably in the absence of any government assistance. Even with government programs, U.S. statistics on farm labor present a clear picture of a decline in the number of agricultural households that depend on farm work for employment. By 1987, close to 70 percent of U.S. agricultural households depended on income from nonfarm employment.[28] Finally, even with off-farm earnings, agricultural households as a group have lower incomes than families nationwide although there are many wealthy farm families.[29]

It is not the structure of farms but the central planning system itself, with its myriad directives and centrally set prices at all stages, that has created an inefficient and costly farm and food delivery system in the former USSR. Until very recently, numerous instructions guided day-to-day farm operation, including when to begin planting or harvesting. Under central planning, no farm was allowed to fail; unprofitable and loss-making farms were subsidized with credits that seldom were repaid. Prices for both resources and products — and the bonus system that encouraged sales of product above plan — were largely set by the center. Investment and resource allocation were also centrally set.

Since Leonid Brezhnev outlined his first major effort to expand farm production in 1965, Soviet planners have allocated more and more farm machinery, agrochemicals, construction materials, and other inputs to accelerate growth in production. From 1970 to 1989, capital stock in agriculture more than tripled and deliveries of fertilizer more than doubled. Nonetheless, farm output, according to official Soviet figures, grew by only 35 percent.[30] As a result, production costs per unit escalated, but under the central planning and allocation system, farm managers had no incentive to hold costs down.

A collective or a state farm should be able to operate efficiently and productively in the proper environment. Westerners who visit Soviet farms agree that even in today's chaotic environment, many farm managers are able to run their farms well despite the handicap of central planning and arbitrarily fixed prices. Other farm managers, however, appear to be intent on "running their own kingdoms" and controlling all aspects of farm life rather than maximizing production and minimizing cost.

The right environment for both productivity (high yields) and efficiency (most economical and effective combination of inputs and product) would include:

• Prices for both inputs and products that are relatively free to respond to supply and demand, thereby helping direct scarce resources to the best return;

• Free access to inputs from many suppliers and a Western-style wholesale system; and

• Freedom to market commodities through a variety of channels.

Achieving efficiency in the current state and collective farm system has also been hampered by a financial system that charges no penalty for extravagant operation. State and collective farms are large communities often including several villages, some with schools and other amenities such as small hospitals, farm-product processing facilities, and other small-scale industries to produce construction materials and consumer goods from local raw materials. Collective farms finance all of these activities, as well as pensions and other social protection from their own funds (including state budget credits). State farms receive more grants from the state for financing amenities and other social expenditures. Credit was always easily available and the central authorities periodically forgave massive debt accumulation. In 1990, for example, the state budget forgave 27 billion rubles of farm debt (40 percent of the total owed by farms) in the first half of the year.[31] Moreover, the budget has been generous in both subsidizing unprofitable farms and paying large bonuses for above-plan production. These elements freed farm managers from the need to consider cost as part of the production process or as a factor in making decisions about rural amenities.

Until a few years ago, most state and collective farms could probably have become fairly effective and efficient if freed from central planning constraints, the emphasis on full employment, and the peculiarities of the financial system.[32] Unfortunately, over the past three to four years, general economic conditions have deteriorated to the extent that even with these changes, the former system would probably not be viable. The breakdown in central control, the declining value of the ruble, rampant inflation — estimated at 2 to 3 percent per week — and rapidly increasing republic and oblast autarky are fostering a marked degree of independence among state and collective farms.[33] Both state and collective farms increasingly are holding on to their production for their own use, to barter, or simply in anticipation of higher prices. Indicative of the breakdown in central control, procurement agencies, which traditionally supplied agricultural raw materials to the processing industry and to the trade network, are finding it steadily becoming more difficult to purchase the planned quantities. In mid-October, procurements of potatoes and other vegetables were roughly 20 percent and 10 percent behind the low 1990 levels, and procurements of grain were lagging by about 40 percent.[34] The extent to which barter transactions between farms, producers of farm inputs and consumer goods, and food processors are increasing is slowly changing state and collective farms into more independent entities.[35] Although central and republic authorities still largely control the distribution of material resources, their ability to direct these flows, as well as the activities of farms, is rapidly eroding. The extent to which traditional channels are being superseded cannot be determined, but anecdotal evidence confirms that they are losing their importance.[36]

Possible Outcomes

The devolution of authority from the former center to the republics, and in some cases to smaller administrative governmental units, and the deterioration of the traditional distribution system indicate that resolving the current disarray in the food production and distribution system cannot be accomplished by the weakened center. Republic cooperation, with or without the center, will also be difficult to achieve as local and republic officials strive to protect their own food supplies. Officials of 10 republics signed a one-year agreement in early October 1991 defining the volume of agricultural raw material and food they expect to import and export in 1992. The agreement also specifies quantities of foreign imports for each republic. Republics that fail to meet their obligations will still have to pay the hard currency (presumably to the state budget) needed to purchase the goods on world markets. The penalty clause suggests this agreement might be more forceful than the Gorbachev-initiated agreement in effect in 1991.[37]

Ukraine — a key food-exporting republic — at first refused to sign but later apparently did so.[38] If Ukraine is serious about cooperating, the agreement may have some success. At the same time, republic authorities will still be faced with acquiring raw materials from farms in their republics. Higher procurement prices and promises of deliveries of scarce goods to farms have generally not been successful in stepping up procurements in 1991.[39] Farms are able to earn the same amount of rubles by selling smaller quantities of grain, and the widespread inability of the central and republic authorities to meet promises of deliveries of scarce goods — construction materials, consumer goods, and the like — for sales to the state beyond the plan quantity has added to farms' reluctance to sell to the state.[40]

At the same time, the increasing independence of state- and collective-farm decision making and the growth of barter transactions, combined with the moves toward land reform, privatization, and reports of the breakup of farms by farm managers in several areas confirm that the traditional state and collective farm structure may be dissolving. Similarly, the increasing use of barter will also eventually dissolve the traditional supply and distribution system. Although barter is a primitive form of trade, it does represent a rudimentary market and establishes free prices of a sort, or at least equivalent exchange. Developing market relations from a centrally-planned system that is reverting to barter, however, would take decades. The current food situation, as well as the overall economic decline, argue that the former Soviet Union, or whatever entity will replace it, must move forcefully toward either reasserting a command economy or toward speeding up the development of relatively free markets for all stages of the food production chain. Either direction would cause serious dislocations and would be painful. As the overall situation deteriorates, the likelihood of a reversion to a command system becomes more remote. Transition to a market system, however, would demand programs to assist favored groups of the population.

What moves would spur the development of market relations? In the macroeconomic sense, one of the key elements is reestablishing financial stability and halting the decline in the ruble's value. A hard budget constraint that ends the current, almost endless, availability of credit is crucial. Increasing wages and procurement prices to compensate for soaring consumer and input prices can only lead to massive budget deficits at both central and republic levels. Hyperinflation is the eventual result. Freeing prices — an essential step — would undoubtedly spur already high inflation. But Poland's experience shows that after a period — a few months in Poland's case — rapid price escalation can slow and even reverse itself. In the former USSR, the process undoubtedly would take longer but would follow the same trend. Making the currency — be it rubles or independent republic monetary units — convertible would initially cause enormous disruption and pain for financial institutions as well as industries, farms, and consumers. If assured of fairly stable value, however, all these entities could relax the compulsion to hoard goods. The longstanding Soviet belief that big is better and that concentration of production in a few locations is more efficient will likely be more difficult and take longer to overcome, in large part because of the enormous existing capital stock and need for new investment. Resolving questions of legal authority, responsibility, and contract sanctity will also be crucial.

Focusing more directly on the microeconomic aspects of the food production and marketing system, a mixture of forms of farm operation is crucial in a country as large and as diverse as the former Soviet Union. Dissolving state and collective farms abruptly would be disastrous. As noted above, many of them are operating well. With relatively free prices and the right to decide what and how to produce, as well as what inputs to buy from which suppliers and a choice of marketing channels, these farms should become as efficient as large, corporate farms in the West. Other state and collective farms could be broken up into their constituent parts and managed separately, perhaps by groups of workers. Smaller livestock operations have already been successfully hived off collective farms, and small family groups are managing and harvesting large areas of grain in several republics. The brigade system, initiated in the 1960s, produced some remarkable results in terms of productivity but was largely discarded because it took on the flavor of campaign; soon everyone was assigned to brigades and the relationship between wages and output was lost.[41] Still other collective farms could develop into true cooperatives in the Western understanding, with shares held by members. A few instances of such changes in the Baltic countries and Kirghizia have already been reported. Their success appears to be dependent on creative management and sympathetic local officials. At the same time, farms that are unprofitable, for whatever reason, must be allowed to go bankrupt rather than being sustained by increasing amounts of credit. In some cases financial restructuring will be sufficient; in others, such as where natural resources are poor, farms should be eliminated.[42]

The role of peasant farms in producing food will expand but will remain relatively small as a share of total output throughout the rest of this decade. Bureaucratic resistence, legislation restricting peasant farm size, the absence of sufficient equipment and other needed inputs, and the lack of desire of individuals to take on the risk and hard work will slow the development of peasant farms. The likelihood of Western-style family farms is even more remote, in part because of the deep-seated ideological bias against private ownership and the purchase and sale of land. The need to develop an infrastructure — ranging from input supply to product marketing to housing and other rural amenities spread over a large area, however, is also an enormous handicap. Overcoming these obstacles could take decades and will be very costly. Moreover, the relative absence of other employment opportunities in rural areas suggests underemployment in these areas will persist for years. Nonetheless, there are signs that resistance to private farming and the jealousy that has led to burned buildings and destroyed equipment is declining as more peasant farms are established.[43]

Producing more food more efficiently on farms of all types and reestablishing financial stability will reduce the budget expenditures that have made the farm sector such a drain on the economy. Achieving this goal requires more than land reform. Similarly, resolving the chronic food problem requires much more than producing more food more efficiently. Eliminating the constraints imposed by central planning and freeing prices throughout the food producing and marketing chain, along with a number of other measures that traditionally were ideologically unacceptable such as arbitrage and hired labor will be required. Land reform, even with its restrictions, must be considered a positive move.

Sources and Notes

1. *Pravda*, 1 April 1989, pp. 1, 3.

2. See, for example, *Komsomolskaya pravda*, 6 March 1991, p. 2.

3. *Glasnost*, no. 7, 14 February 1991, pp. 1-3, provides several examples.

4. *Izvestiya*, 18 April 1991, p. 1.

5. V. N. Semenov, *Ekonomika sel'skokhozyaystvennykh i pererabatyvayushchikh predpriatiy*, September 1990, p.7.

6. Based on state and collective farm data presented in official Soviet publications such as *Narodnoye khozyaystvo SSSR v 1989g*, (hereafter Nkh and the year) Moscow, 1990, pp. 436-443, 503, 511, and earlier editions.

7. Judith Flynn and Barbara Severin, "Soviet Agricultural Transport: Bottlenecks to Continue," in *Gorbachev's Economic Plans*, Volume 2, Joint Economic Committee, Congress of the United States, November 23, 1987, pp. 62-78.

8. *Ibid*, pp. 77-78.

9. *Nkh 85*, pp. 187, 202, and earlier editions. In the former USSR private agricultural production traditionally was permitted only on rural "private plots" and suburban "garden plots," cultivated mainly by city dwellers. Foodstuffs are produced for the plot owners' use. Surplus can be sold through collective farm markets or to the various state procurement agencies. Nearly all collective farm families and about 80 percent of other rural families — close to 36 million households — have plots that range from one-half to one acre. At the end of 1989, nearly 20 million families belonged to "horticultural organizations" and had garden plots averaging three-tenths of an acre according to *SSSR v tsifrakh v 1990*, Moscow, 1991, p. 242.

10. *Nkh 87*, p. 217.

11. *Nkh 87*, p. 226, and *Sel'skokhozyaystvennoye proizvodstvo v lichnykh podsobnykh khozyaystvakh naseleniya*, Moscow, 1989, p. 29.

12. Individuals can hold land and farm it very effectively and efficiently without owning it by leasing either long- or short-term and even by renting year-to-year as often is the case in the United States. To do so, of course, requires that farmers are free to make their own management decisions and that prices for both inputs and products are relatively free.

13. See, for example, Gorbachev's speeches at the Fourth All-Union Congress of Kolkhozviks in Moscow, March 1988. Earlier, Moscow's rumor mill credited Gorbachev with the January 1981 legislation that legalized contracts between farms and plot holders primarily for production of meat and milk. The legislation can be found in *Sel'skaya zhizn'*, 18 January 1981, p. 1.

14. *Izvestiya*, 7 March 1990, pp. 1-2.

15. *Pravda*, 10 March 1990, p. 4. Also in March 1990, the Supreme Soviet approved a controversial law on property rights that broadened the definition of "socialist" property to include both public and individual ownership. As defined, the property law does not include land. The legislation can be found in *Ekonomika i zhizn'* no. 30 July 1991 Supplement, p. 2.

16. *Glasnost*, no. 4, 1991, p. 4.

17. *Christian Science Monitor*, 20 May 1991.

18. *Sovetskaya Rossiya*, 21 February 1991, p. 1.

19. *Nkh 89*, pp. 501-502, 509-510.

20. Yeltsin on Moscow TV, 28 October 1991.

21. See, for example, *Izvestiya*, 25 February 1991, p.4.

22. Roy Prosterman and Timothy Hanstad, *An Update on Individual Peasant Farming in the USSR*, RDI Monograph on Foreign Aid and Development, no. 8, October 1991, p. 43.

23. Reuters, Moscow, 16 October 1991.

24. Russian television, 1800 GMT, 18 October 1991.

25. Alexander Meyendorff, "Moscow letter," *RSEEA, Research on Soviet and East European Agriculture*, Vol. 13, Issue 3, September 1991, pp. 3-5.

26. *Agricultural Statistics 1988*, U.S. Department of Agriculture, (Washington, D. C.: U.S. GPO, 1988), p. 371. State farms in the USSR average 30,000 acres and collective farms about 13,000 acres according to *Nkh 89*, pp. 501-502, 509-510.

27. Ibid p. 373.

28. "Characteristics of Agricultural Work Force Households, 1987," U.S. Department of Agriculture, Economic Research Service, Agriculture Information Bulletin Number 612, August 1990, p. 5.

29. "The Farm Entrepreneurial Population, 1988," U.S. Department of Agriculture, Economic Research Service, Rural Development Research Report Number 78, July 1990, p. 11.

30. *Nkh 89*, pp. 277, 416, 483, *Nkh 85*, p. 180, *Nkh 82*, pp. 46, 232.

31. *Ekonomika i zhizn'*, no. 29, 1990, p. 3.

32. Some farms are located in areas that should not be farmed. Grain farms, for example, east of the Urals in areas that do not return more than seed for the following year in two out of three years should be eliminated.

33. Grigory Yavlinsky, in *Rossiyskaya gazeta*, 14 September 1991, p. 1, commented that inflation has hit 2-3 percent per week.

34. Moscow, TASS International Service, 16 October 1991, *Sel'skaya zhizn'*, 18 October 1991.

35. Prosterman and Hanstad, op.cit., p.19

36. *New York Times*, 4 September 1991, p. A1. *Pravda*, 19 August 1991, p. 1.

37. *Izvestiya*, 10 October 1991, p. 2.

38. Interfax, Moscow, 6 November 1991.

39. *Rossiyskaya gazeta*, 15 October 1991, p. 1.

40. *Izvestiya*, 26 July 1991, p. 2. Procurements of grain in 1991 were roughly 60 percent of the 1990 total, the lowest in five decades.

41. Don Van Atta "Why Do Models Succeed," in *Communist Agriculture, Farming in the Soviet Union and Eastern Europe*, edited by Karl-Eugen Wädekin, (New York: Routledge, 1990), pp. 185-201.

42. Cook, Edward, "Uncertainties Over Reform: Decentralization or Recentralization," ibid,. pp. 132-135.

43. Prosterman and Hanstad, op. cit., pp. 43-46.

10

Essential Roles of the Government in Agriculture

Allan Mustard

W e are seeing today a potential revolution in the government's role in agriculture in the Soviet Union. Since May 1991, three, high-level United States Department of Agriculture delegations have travelled to the "former Union" to assess Soviet food problems and to determine what kind of assistance the Soviets need and how it can be rendered. The delegations visited Moscow, St. Petersburg, Kiev, Minsk, Alma Ata, Tashkent, Yerevan, Ufa, Stavropol, Yekaterinburg, and Samarkand. In most places we were asked what role the government should play in the agricultural sector and to discuss the U.S. government's agricultural programs and philosophy. My discussion looks at government intervention in the agricultural sector in this context: What does the U.S. government do? What has the Soviet government traditionally done? What models do we have that we might share with the Soviets?

The Essential Roles of Government

In its broadest sense, governments of all types share two sets of necessary functions. There are functions the private sector cannot or will not perform, and functions the public sector can perform more efficiently, effectively, or fairly. Most sovereign jurisdictions have long recognized that the first category includes such responsibilities as coining money, waging war, maintaining public order and safety, and building public roads. Even these are subject to exceptions: banks open checking accounts, thus creating

Opinions expressed herein are those of the author and do not necessarily reflect official positions of the United States government.

money; non-sovereign terrorist groups wage guerilla warfare; private security firms and ambulances abound; and private toll roads have existed for centuries.

The question becomes even murkier when one examines the second category, those functions a government can theoretically perform more efficiently: regulation of commerce, price stabilization, maintenance of economic stability, education, research, and information dissemination. For every example of governmental success in preventing a Bunkie Hunt from cornering the silver market, there is a Salomon Brothers which succeeded in cornering the securities market; for every economy that has kept inflation from getting out of control, there is or has been an Israel or Weimar Republic with hyperinflation.

Roles of the American Government

Essential roles of government in agriculture can be argued until the cows come home. U.S. government policy in American agriculture has been shaped since a farmer, George Washington, was the nation's first president. It has tended toward the free market. Significant federal intervention began in the mid-1800s and intensified during the Great Depression. The degree of government intervention in American agriculture is perhaps best typified by the size of the Food, Agriculture, Conservation and Trade Act of 1990, known as the 1990 Farm Bill. The 450-page act defines what the Administration will do in agriculture for the next five years, from tobacco farm supports in the Carolinas to support of dairy farms in California. U.S. government involvement in agriculture covers a wide range of activities ranging from food stamps for Americans living in poverty to food donations to Africans in danger of starvation, from rural telephones to crop insurance to disaster relief, from soil conservation to promotion of exports to assuring food safety to consumers, from dealing with the northern spotted hoot owl in the Pacific Northwest to the gypsy moth along the eastern seaboard to the screw worm in Mexico and the Colorado potato beetle worldwide.

The lead agency of the U.S. government in agriculture is the United States Department of Agriculture, created in 1862 by President Abraham Lincoln. Other federal agencies involved in governmental agricultural policy making and implementation include the U.S. Departments of Health and Human Services, Interior, State, Commerce, and Treasury; the Environmental Protection Agency, and the Office of Management and Budget. The basic goal of the Government has not changed dramatically over time:

the assurance of stable supplies of food, fiber, and raw materials within the overall framework of a relatively free market.

This goal, however, has justified myriad programs. Price stabilization and farm income assurance, for example, are specific goals that have led to crop set-aside programs, whereby farmers are paid not to grow food or are paid subsidized prices to produce commodities which in a given year may suffer from depressed prices. Supply assurance concerns, in turn, have led to subsidies for production of sugar, a strategic commodity which the continental U.S. does not produce competitively or cheaply.

Concerns about stability of supply have spawned research institutions in cooperation with universities and colleges. This system disseminates research findings, as well as unbiased information that keeps farmers, processors, merchants, and consumers abreast of market conditions.

Consumer nutrition, environmental affairs, and export promotion are three, relatively new directions for U.S. government intervention. When I say relatively, I mean this century. Virtually every county in the United States has had an extension home economist (a USDA employee advising home-makers on proper nutrition, food handling, and preparation) for decades. Today this effort has expanded into feeding programs, product labelling, consumer protection, and nutritional assistance. Federal environmental programs are rooted in concerns dating back to the 19th century about soil erosion, overgrazing, and renewal of timber resources. Today these con-cerns have expanded to encompass endangered species, a reduction in water quality due to pesticide and fertilizer runoff, land use planning, and increasingly scarce water resources.

The last of the three new directions is export promotion. America has exported grain, timber, and cotton for centuries, but only in the last 40 years has the federal government significantly promoted American agriculture abroad. During the 1980s, the United States exported 30 percent of its corn, over 50 percent of its rice, cotton, and soybeans, and 60 percent of its wheat and wheat flour. From another perspective, U.S. wheat accounts for roughly one-third of world trade in that commodity; it also accounts for half the world trade in feed grains, half to two-thirds of the trade in soybeans, and a quarter to a third of the trade in cotton. There are USDA officials in about 70 countries around the world whose major task is to promote U.S. agricultural products and to report on market conditions. We also operate export market promotion programs, offer credit guarantees, and wage diplomatic battle with countries that maintain barriers to our exports.

The focus of these programs remains, however, the support of a free market system, not the supplanting of it. The U.S. government seeks not to run the market, or to be the market, but to ensure that it will function in the best interests of the public. Those interests are defined quite specifically every five years by Congress, a body of elected officials, in the Farm Bill.

Traditional Roles of the Soviet Government

Let's contrast U.S. philosophy with that of the Soviet government until 1990. Lenin said, "Grain is the currency of currencies." With that in mind, one of the first things the Soviet state did was to take control of grain supplies, by confiscating grain and other foods in the 1920s. This was followed by collectivization in the 1930s. Unlike the United States, where grain is stored largely either on the farm or at transportation nodes, the Soviets established food storage at points of end use — the cities.

The rationale for this was political. If a Communist system was to be forced on the peasantry against its will, the peasantry had to be rendered powerless. The peasantry's only weapon was the food it produced. Forced confiscations, which were eventually replaced by quota-based mandatory state procurements, coupled with prohibitions on storage on the farm, denied political power to the countryside and transferred it to the urban-based Communists.

The Communist political leadership also sought to control all aspects of the market. This included inputs such as machinery, motor fuel and lubricants, fertilizer, pesticides, and labor. Prices were strictly controlled for these items. Access was possible only through the political leadership. Production was largely dictated by the Communist Party, based on central planning and oft-unrealistic targets. Prices for food and fiber products were also set by the state; the system featured retail prices set lower than procurement and wholesale prices. Artificially low retail prices, in turn, led to massive government subsidies and chronic shortages of many foodstuffs.

Food distribution was largely in public hands as well. The state owned and operated centralized warehouses and grain elevators, as well as retail stores. It also controlled everything else in between, including transportation, processing, and packaging. Investment was wholly centrally planned and focused on production at the expense of post-harvest processing.

The Bolshevik government and its successors also took up many of the other functions found in Western market economies, but often with a twist. Much emphasis has been placed on research, but research that answered the needs of the political leadership. Economic researchers whose theories conflicted with those of Stalin were arrested in 1930 and shot in 1937, including such brilliant men as N.D. Kondratyev, author of the Kondratyev wave theory, and A.V. Chayanov, one of this century's most gifted researchers on markets and peasant agriculture. The biologist N.I. Vavilov was ousted as president of the Agricultural Academy of Sciences, and his works were discredited. The government promoted his successor, the notorious T.D. Lysenko, because his work on acquired characteristics fit the political concept of creating a new Soviet man.

In one very limited sense, the Soviet government succeeded in stabilizing prices, since retail prices were stable from 1961 to 1989. This official policy is now on the road to being removed, but the effects of years of suppressed inflation are now manifesting themselves in an inflationary spiral. Some officials in Moscow told our delegation in October 1991 that they expect inflation to rise to five percent per week by early 1992, or more than 1,000 percent per year. This is hyperinflation, and hardly qualifies as a price stabilization policy.

It is fair to say that the Soviet government's agricultural and food policy has been an unqualified disaster. Today, the national leadership has its hand outstretched for foreign aid and credits, admits that the agricultural infrastructure is on the verge of collapse, and concedes that the system desperately needs reform. Despite an abundance of natural resources, a highly literate and educated population, and cropping conditions no worse than those found in Canada — a grain exporting nation — the Soviet government's role in agriculture has brought the nation to its knees. What lessons can we learn from this? Can some of the U.S. experience in the government's role in agriculture be applied to the reform process now underway in the Soviet Union?

Prospects for Soviet Transition

The past year has witnessed a turnabout of startling rapidity as the Soviet Union's government has repudiated Marxian socialism and has philosophically embraced a transition to market economics. However, two major obstacles impede transition to a market. The first is continued foot-dragging and opposition to the transition by mid-level bureaucrats and former wheels in the Communist Party. This includes collective and state farm managers, whose interests until August 22, 1991, were represented by Vasily Starodubtsev. (Starodubstev, a farm manager and chairman of the conservative Peasants' Union, was a member of the August coup junta and is now in prison.) This class has the most to lose, for in a market economy there is much less need for bureaucrats who order farmers when and what to sow, till and reap, as well as set prices, control the flow of merchandise, and in general exert control over the economy. The only layer of this bureaucracy that seems to have disappeared, incidentally, is the Young Communist League. Its assets and personnel appear to have been reborn largely as a series of commercial firms and holding companies, run by former Young Communists. Removal of this obstacle at the middle level may only be possible by buying off the bureaucrats.

The second obstacle is ignorance. The Soviet Union has by and large been insular for 60 years, and most of the leadership, for that matter most of the population, has never been exposed to Western economic management. This was brought home by a recent conversation with a Soviet agricultural official who asked how many hours a day the U.S. Secretary of Agriculture spends ensuring that food supplies are delivered to New York.

None, I assured him; the private sector with its profit motive seeks to sell as much as it can in America's largest city and thus takes care of New York's demand for food without federal interference. Impossible, he responded, what else does the Secretary do if not that? Our Minister of Agriculture and Food, he assured me, worries about getting food delivered to Moscow every day, and appropriately so.

These two obstacles mean that there is great opposition to change at the working level, but even worse, Soviet policy makers don't know what they want to change to. Prospects are not bright for a smooth transition in a land where privatizing an enterprise can mean the state retains a controlling share of the assets, and where state price controls are unraveling only because there is almost nothing available through the state retail network.

Lessons From U.S. Agriculture

What lessons can be drawn from the U.S. agricultural system for helping the Soviets make a transition? Let's look at the major tasks the Soviets face. The first task is privatization of capital and land. Without private ownership, without some form of collateralization, money cannot be invested, borrowed, or loaned in the private sector. Second is decentralization of decision making. In conversations with republic-level officials, with only a few exceptions, decentralization has meant moving the decisions from Moscow to the republic capital. This is not decentralization as you and I know it. Decentralization, meaning the authority to make economic decisions at the enterprise level, is a critical need.

Third is a wholesale restructuring of the production and distribution sectors and the creation of production, processing, storage, transportation, and marketing enterprises and institutions of suitable scale. The Soviets do recognize the need to step away from Stalin's gigantism mania, and some even recognize the need to empower the small entrepreneur. They don't know how markets function, however, and are deeply suspicious of using prices to adjust supply and demand. In fact, a certain level of suspicion may be justified in the short run as gigantism has led to local monopolies which could crush competition and distort markets. For lack of a better term, we might call this a need for proper scale.

A fourth issue is tax revenues. The Soviet government is worse than bankrupt. It is so deep in the hole that it can only finance itself by printing money, and the major constraint on printing new money is how fast the presses can churn out new banknotes. The Soviet government is now financed by turnover taxes, which are a share of the profits from state enterprises, plus a five-percent "presidential" tax levied on retail sales. As the economy is privatized, revenues from that source will fall. Revenues are already declining to the point where many government officials have sidelines, operated out of their offices, to make ends meet both at home and at work. Central budget allocations are insufficient to cover office expenses and salaries, and official salaries are lagging far behind inflation. Within this context, then, a major remaining issue is defining a new role for the central and republic governments in agriculture.

Thus we have five key issues: privatization, decentralization, proper scaling, revenue generation, and redefining a role for government. What can the United States offer? We can offer continued moral support and assurance that the market can, overall, be trusted. Marketization of the Soviet economy will inescapably lead to resolution of the first three issues and provide a basis for resolving the fourth. Privatized farming, food processing, and merchandising are vastly more efficient and effective than any state-run counterparts. The U.S. role in these areas is largely a regulatory one, and I emphasize again that the U.S. government does not make decisions on what to plant, when to harvest, or what tractors to use.

Let me digress with an illustration. In the spring of 1991, the Minister of Grain Products of one of the republics visited Washington and called on the Deputy Undersecretary of Agriculture. He asked him how many employees the USDA had (over 100,000), then asked who among them tells the farmer what to grow. The Underecretary described for 10 minutes the meaning of loan rates and set asides, then closed with the comment that USDA programs affect only a few commodities, and that the bulk are subject to market forces. The Minister scowled, and responded, "You obviously misunderstood my question. I will ask again. Who tells the farmers what to grow?"

The answer, of course, is that prices and their relationships across commodities tell the farmer what to grow in America, and while the U.S. government sets a floor price for certain commodities to ensure a minimal return to the farmer, it does not dictate prices nor does it demand that anybody buy or sell at a particular price (an exception to that is dairy products, but they can be considered here as the exception that proves the rule). By setting an artificially high support price for sugar beets, the U.S. government assures that in time of war domestic sugar will be available, but it does not dictate that any particular farmer will grow sugar beets. On the other hand, prices of meats, fruits and vegetables, and potatoes fluctuate with the market. The United States can share this experience in limited market intervention with the Soviets as they grope their way toward privatization and a more rational price policy. Coupled with this must be a dismantling of the Soviet central bureaucracies and transfer of their authority to the private sector.

Incidentally, privatization does not necessarily mean peasantization of agricultural production. While establishing family-sized small holdings may be appropriate in certain areas of the former Union, it is not necessarily appropriate everywhere. We were told in Bashkiria, for example, that the Bashkiri and Tatars have no legacy of individual private ownership and were leaning toward communal ownership of property. The Don Cossacks of Rostov oblast voiced similar opinions. In principle, private farming is not completely incompatible with corporate ownership, as experience in the United States can attest.

Decentralized Decision Making Is Essential

The question of privatization leads to the second issue, decentralization in decision making. In the United States, decisions are made at the local level; farmers, middlemen, and retailers make their own determinations about producing, buying, selling, and pricing. This step will be one of the hardest for the Soviets. Those with power will not easily relinquish it, and those unaccustomed to individual authority will at least initially find it difficult to exercise. People have to learn how to make decisions, and an individual who has been told all his professional life what to do has no experience in decision making. A side issue to this is that, historically, the penalties for showing initiative or making incorrect decisions in the Soviet Union have been exceedingly high. The United States can direct assistance to the Soviet Union in training decision makers at the farm and firm level. Assuming that the bureaucrats have been disenfranchised by privatization and marketization, devolution of decision making will naturally follow.

The proper scaling of infrastructure is the next area where we have experience. This is a long-term problem for the Soviets. First, capital infrastructure, by its nature, is built for the long haul. It is not built with the expectation that one day it will be torn down and broken up into smaller parts. Second, much of the Soviet infrastructure is worn out; it will be costly and time-consuming to replace it.

Another problem is that the Soviets sometimes don't realize that they are acting illogically in the context of a market economy. In the United States, we build excess capacity into processing facilities so that products can be processed before they deteriorate or rot. Our facilities are designed to handle peak capacities, and do so because the market demands a high-quality product and firm owners demand profitability. To us, spoiled product equals lost profits.

Soviet government policy, on the other hand, has created bottlenecks in processing. Facilities are not designed for peak loading. They are designed to run for a long processing season to provide full employment. If a product rots in a warehouse waiting to be processed, if tomatoes sit in a truck for 48 hours awaiting unloading, if cotton waits 11 months to be ginned and turns bad in the interim, it has, up until now, been in the name of full employment and social welfare. This is only one example of improper scales. Another involves warehousing fruits and vegetables. Because the Soviet government promoted gigantism, the entire city of Moscow, with nine million people and an array of state-owned green grocers, hospitals, orphanages, and rest homes, is served by 16 vegetable and fruit warehouses. Because fruits and vegetables are in short supply, the 16 warehouse directors exert considerable influence. They, and not the market, determine which institutions will receive produce and which will go begging. In a competitive market, there would be more warehouses that would compete against each other to provide services and quality products.

Here again, the United States can share some expertise in resolving a longer-term issue. The U.S. government encourages investment in business facilities with tax breaks and benefits and helps small entrepreneurs with loans. The Soviets have virtually no experience with taxation policy and its role in promoting business development. We can also advise their emerging commodity exchanges and capital markets and help them develop appropriate regulatory mechanisms to protect investors and consumers. Here the Soviets face the particular danger of trying to overregulate the new exchanges; a good dose of free-market capitalism is in order here as in no other sector of the economy. The promotion of ruble investment in infrastructure would have the added bonus of drawing rubles out of circulation and putting them to some use other than chasing consumer goods. This comes back to the issue of privatization, of assuring the Soviets that it is a proper course, and of sharing technical expertise to get new economic mechanisms and institutions in place and functioning. This in time will lead to more efficient structuring of physical infrastructure, as economic criteria overtake the political criteria of the past.

This brings up the fourth point, which is taxation itself. I hate to admit this, but the Soviets really need a revenue service. If the economy is privatized, the Soviet government will need a source of revenue. If a price support system is adopted along the lines of the U.S. system, it will have to be funded. An extension service, along the U.S. or one of the European models, would also have to be funded. If commodity exchanges and capital markets are to be monitored for miscreants, that, too, will have to be funded. I doubt that anybody will deny that the U.S. government has a fair amount of experience in levying taxes.

The final point, defining a new role for whatever government is responsible for agricultural policy, comes naturally. If we look to the U.S. government as a model, we see that it has historically supported the private sector. This includes educating farmers and agribusinessmen; conducting research; providing market infrastructure the private sector cannot or will not provide, including market-oriented statistical and economic analysis; quarantine and inspection; promoting environmental quality; facilitating rural development; assuming some of the excessive risk involved in agricultural production; and providing nutritional assistance to the needy. These are appropriate areas for a government which intends to transfer productive assets and control of those assets to a private sector.

Let me close with a picture taken in early October 1991 on Novy Arbat in downtown Moscow. It shows a man saying he is ready to bake bread, another is ready to open a store, another says he is ready to sell at a profit, and a fourth is ready to found a joint venture. The gray sign at the bottom in the middle of a desolate field says, "And who is ready to grow it?" The answer, of course, is that given a proper incentive and a proper profit motive, many people will be ready to grow grain, or any other agricultural product. American agriculture does this every year. Government plays only a subsidiary, supporting role in a cast of characters where the private sector plays the lead.

11

Russian Agriculture Between Plan and Market

Don Van Atta

Since the 1930s, overlapping administrative hierarchies extending from the central party and state authorities in Moscow to the smallest farm production squad have controlled Soviet agriculture. The limits of economic activity are ultimately set politically in all societies since governmental action determines currencies, legal structures, national boundaries, and other features of the economic "playing field." But the extreme fusion of political organs and economic administration has been a unique feature of the Soviet-type political system. Attempts to limit the Soviet political system's economic functions, the authorities' loss of will to use coercive force against the population, and the citizens' own realization that they could safely ignore the state's orders led to the collapse of governmental authority.

The large collective and state farms originated as political devices to control the peasantry. The coercive methods developed to manage those farms were then adapted to the rest of the economy. For any transformation of the overall Stalinist "command-administrative system" to succeed, agricultural administration must be changed. Reforming the existing agrarian order in the former Soviet Union requires two separate, but logically connected, sets of structural changes. First, production, land-holding, and property relations as they affect individual farm workers must be altered within the existing collective and state farms.[1] As a result of internal changes, individual peasant farms are beginning to develop alongside the kolkhozy and sovkhozy. Second, the economic and political environment in which all Soviet farms operate must be recreated through the development of new supply, marketing, and service arrangements. They have also begun to appear in the former USSR, although they have received less attention than the development of small farms.

This paper examines only the second set of reforms, changes in the farms' environment.[2] It begins by sketching the standard Soviet system for agricultural management and supply that existed in its essentials from the 1930s until the late 1980s. It then outlines the "cooperative alternative," proposed in the late 1980s as part of perestroika, and describes some of the best-publicized models of these new organizations. These "cooperatives" preserved the state's monopoly control over the farms, however. Only competing supply, processing, marketing, and other services can really give farmers incentives to increase and improve production and assure them freedom from the remnants of the old totalitarian system. So the paper next examines how competitive structures linking farms and the national economy are beginning to be developed.

The concluding section examines the political implications of these developments. (Although the old model applied uniformly throughout the former Soviet Union, the discussion of reforms applies primarily to the Russian republic.) A viable national government can only reemerge when the economic mechanisms which knit together farms, suppliers, processors, and markets have been separated from the old administrative hierarchy and reconstructed. This process must proceed locally and regionally, not from the "center" out as agrarian reforms in the Russian Empire and the USSR have traditionally done.

The Management of Soviet Command Agriculture

By the mid-1930s, a standard model of agricultural organization, codified in the "kolkhoz model charter" adopted at the Second Congress of Collective Farmers in 1935, was imposed throughout the USSR. Within the farms, peasant households were replaced as the dominant production and consumption units by large "brigades" in which peasants worked as individuals and were paid according to their work. The brigades were given daily assignments by brigade leaders who in turn received their tasks from higher authorities. The farms themselves were strictly and directly controlled by district and oblast party and state functionaries, who tended to bypass the farm management almost entirely during those times of the agricultural year most critical for food production and procurement.[3] Basic operations were initiated by the political authorities, who annually organized "campaigns" for such tasks as equipment repair, sowing, feed preparation, harvesting, and cattle wintering.

From the 1930s until November 1991, two, parallel, overlapping and competing administrative hierarchies extended from the individual farm production brigade to Moscow.[4] One belonged to the Communist Party of the Soviet Union, the other to the Soviet government. Communist Party dominance had at least four sources. First was the party's *nomenklatura* power of appointment and removal of personnel throughout the party and state.[5] Second was party discipline, effected in the party committees' ability to give party punishments to managers. Too many reprimands would certainly stop career advancement and often cost one one's job. Third was the party member's immunity from state prosecution. Party members had to be thrown out of the party before they could be prosecuted. Crimes, such as the bribery and corruption needed to make any enterprise work, could not be punished unless the manager had his party card taken away. Fourth was the finely calibrated system of access to privileges and scarce goods. Privilege depended on one's job. The job depended on the party. So the party's manipulation of its personnel powers governed who had what privileges. This was a powerful lever in a society where all goods were scarce, and all paths of upward mobility were controlled by the party apparatus. Although Russian President Boris Yeltsin formally outlawed the Russian and All-Union Communist Parties in the wake of the August 1991 coup attempt, Yeltsin's own presidential plenipotentiaries assigned to each region of the RSFSR still carry out most of the party's old administrative functions.

The government apparatus itself has usually had three competing parts: one set of agencies providing production inputs for the farms; another group managing farm operations; and a third collecting, storing, processing, and shipping farm products to the cities. Inputs and management have usually been the concern of the Ministry of Agriculture. A separate Ministry of State Farms has existed intermittently, splitting responsibility for production management with the agricultural ministry (which then retained responsibility only for the collective farms). The Ministry of Procurements and the Ministry of the Food Industry have usually been separate from the agriculture ministry.

Stalinist agricultural policy sought maximum control over the farms by manipulating their linkages to suppliers and markets. Machinery, spare parts, and fuel were provided through a network of state "Machine-Tractor Stations" (MTS), administered by a separate unit of the Ministry of Agriculture. Collective farms paid for MTS' operations in produce, making the stations the most important lever for extracting farm products for the cities during most of the Stalin era. Nikita Khrushchev abandoned this system of separating farm equipment operations from the farms, selling the Machine-Tractor Stations' equipment to the kolkhozy. Farms were forced to buy all the MTS equipment, whether a particular farm wished to or not, at state-set prices. The debts farms incurred while buying out the MTS in the late 1950s were written off in 1965. But a new monopoly of repair facilities, agricultural equipment sales, and spare-part supplies, the State Committee for Material-Technical Supply of Agriculture (*Sel'khoztekhnika*), replaced the old MTS. Farms were still forced to deal with their local branch of the state committee. Since the new agencies received plans for volume and/or value of sales, inexpensive but needed spare parts such as belts were virtually unobtainable, and farms frequently had to pay for unnecessary repairs or buy useless equipment in order to get a needed repair or new machine. In the late 1980s, Sel'khoztekhnika in turn was reorganized into the Agricultural Supply Association (Agrosnab). But the new supply agency remained a part of the Ministry of Agriculture, and its local branches retained their monopolies.

Although Khrushchev also abolished the old system of paying produce for mechanized work, the state retained its monopoly over procurements. After the late 1950s, farms were simply given plans for delivery of their crops to the local procurement agency. The state still monopolized the purchase of farms' above-plan output though it paid a premium for such deliveries. A state-sanctioned "cooperative" monopoly purchased private plot output for resale — and this "Central Consumers' Cooperative" had its plan assignment for the volume of foodstuffs it would purchase. This *Tsentrosoiuz* also handled much of the distribution of processed foods and consumer goods in the countryside, so its local branches sometimes required peasants to sell it produce before allowing them to buy other goods. The state continued to set purchase prices unilaterally, so that farms' production costs and income from produce sales frequently did not balance, leaving farms in debt to the state. The plan targets were renamed "state orders" (*goszakazy*) in 1987, but they have continued to be obligatory commands given to the farms.

Stalin forbade local food processing and what the Chinese term "sideline industries" on the farms in the 1930s. Even hand mills for grinding grain were confiscated and destroyed during collectivization. In order to maximize the amount of produce extracted from the farms, storage and processing facilities have been built off the farms in district centers. Large food-storage warehouses ("bases") were built on the outskirts of large cities. Unlike wholesale markets in the United States, these bases were designed for the long-term storage of food products, including fruits and vegetables. As a result, large quantities of produce spoil in storage — most Soviet students and many white-collar workers have been mobilized to sort out rotten produce at a city warehouse, a job people dislike even more than the periodic treks to the farms to get the harvest in. Centralized storage also made Soviet cities vulnerable. A single chance German bomb on the main food warehouse in Leningrad destroyed more than a year's stocks of food for the city in the fall of 1941. As a result, the city starved through the winter of 1941-42, the first year of the 900-day siege of the city during World War II.

Farms themselves had to build internal roads and keep up main roads on their territory. Until the 1950s, kolkhozy were forbidden to connect into the national electrical grid. Until the 1970s, little state investment was available for rural housing or amenities, and food processing industries received little support until the late 1980s. As a result, transportation, storage, and processing enterprises are not only poorly located, requiring long hauls from the farms, but also insufficient and old.

Farms produced what the plan demanded and delivered their produce to the state. The state allocated production inputs at official monopoly prices in return for kolkhoz production. But getting the right to obtain a scarce, but needed, item (and all possible items have been scarce from the viewpoint of the individual farm) from the monopoly suppliers has been more important than having the money to pay for it. The state bank would eventually supply the money, but money without an allocation order could buy nothing.

Some of the worst effects of these policies were recognized by the mid-1960s, when the Leonid Brezhnev-Aleksei Kosygin leadership team succeeded Khrushchev. They adopted a policy of forgiving farm debts to the state, absorbing wage and pension costs (state pensions for kolkhozniki were introduced in the late 1960s), and steadily raising procurement prices to increase production. The promised, domestic agricultural improvements were limited by drought, waste, and diversion of new investment to bureaucratically independent "partners" of the farms such as land reclamation and agricultural-machinery sales and repair agencies. The farms and their "partners" were all caught in rapid price inflation during the 1970s, fueled in part by the injection of massive state investment into an agricultural sector ill-equipped to absorb it. The recipients of this largesse were largely representatives of the defense and heavy industry constituency that Brezhnev favored. Farms' productivity improved slowly and at great cost during the 1970s, and the policy of massive agricultural investment and foreign food purchases to make up shortfalls became a constant feature of Soviet life. By 1982, despite the capital investments, most farms had become unprofitable by Soviet accounting measures, and only steep new increases in state purchase prices adopted at the May 1982 CPSU Central Committee plenum allowed most farms to show a paper profit.

By the early 1980s, Soviet agriculture was caught in a peculiarly vicious circle. Increasing capital investment led to higher-cost production as much

or more than it increased gross output. Farms were still managed as they had
been in the 1930s, but the good farmers who had not been deported during
collectivization itself as "class enemies" had long since packed up for the
cities.[7] Lack of investment in rural development and the preferential norms
for food distribution applied in the major cities drew many young people to
town. Large areas of central and northern Russian farmland had lost almost
all their able-bodied workers. The resulting hyperurbanization increased
demand for city food supplies. The remaining peasants had never been
interested in doing more than the unavoidable minimum of work on the
collective or state farm's fields. In the 1970s, able to make a relatively decent
living from their guaranteed wages for fulfilling piece-rate operations even
if the harvest failed, most peasants grew more reliant on purchased foodstuffs. They were less and less interested in the drudgery of cultivating their
own plots. As a result, overall available food supplies failed to keep up with
demand.

None of the post-Khrushchev economic stimuli really gave incentives
for increased production. Peasants worked to fulfill their piece-rates, not
market crops. A good farm would still find itself liable for the failures of its
poorer neighbors, so no wise manager would ever work to capacity. "Smart"
managers might deliberately ruin their farms in order to get lower plans and
higher state subsidies.[8] Nor, despite reams of resolutions on farm independence, could farms make their own decisions about what to produce, how
to produce it, where to get the needed inputs, or where to sell it.

Perestroika intensified these perverse dynamics. As industrial enterprises have been forced by reform to show profits, they have repeatedly
increased the prices farms must pay for their production inputs. As a result
of the pressure on the large farms, profitability was reportedly falling
sharply once again by the end of the decade. By the end of 1989 Vasily
Starodubtsev, leader of the USSR Peasants' Union, the farm managers'
organization, demanded that the state channel all new investment to the
farms and recontrol the price of agricultural inputs to maintain large-farm
profitability. Following his recommendations would, of course, only fuel
inflation further by requiring the state to increase its budget deficit—
especially since past performance suggests that the kolkhozy and sovkhozy
are unlikely to efficiently use increased resources to produce more. At the
same time, as industrial wages have increased, more and more money is
chasing a limited quantity of consumer goods, primarily foodstuffs, so that
apparent demand for foodstuffs is increasing rapidly.[9]

The key, off-farm agencies for agricultural management are the rural
district (rayon) authorities. Much of the responsibility for running command agriculture falls on them because of their control of management

decisions and the local and regional party committees' ability to locate scarce inputs for their farms through party channels. S. Verevkin, a kolkhoz chairman from Kursk oblast, describes the responsibilities of the district authorities: distribution of state orders and assurance of the requisite resources for those orders; verification of the use of credits and distribution of priority directions of investment; supply of technical material to the subunit and help in selling their products; territorial planning (without dictation!); the development of agricultural branches; and the locating of processing enterprises. In addition, district authorities monitored land use for the preservation of fertility and coordinated the operations of state services, such as veterinary, quarantine, and equipment inspection.[10]

Although the rayon party organizations are now to be disbanded in the RSFSR, many of their personnel have followed the lead of the district first secretaries and shifted to work for the Soviet (governmental) apparatus. As long as farms continue to operate in an administered economy, as long as no farms can be allowed to liquidate themselves because the farm is the only available provider of social services and welfare for the local population, and as long as there is no competition in providing farms with production inputs, some similar apparatus will continue to exist and operate, whether it is called the party committee or the district agricultural department.

Most attempts to change the farms' environment during the 1980s have concentrated on the district level. The most important pre-perestroika effort to rationalize and improve the farms' environment was the creation of the rayon agroindustrial association (RAPO) to unite all the various supply, processing, production, storage, and construction agencies in a single rural district. Ordered to be generally adopted at the May 1982 CPSU Central Committee plenum, the RAPOs failed to solve the problems of poor coordination and excessive administrative structures.

The Cooperative Alternatives

The farms still face monopoly suppliers for almost any input they might need. On the output side, food processing, distribution, and sales are also in the hands of territorial monopolies. In addition, many kolkhozy and sovkhozy are kept alive only by bank loans and artificial price subsidies. Especially in the Russian heartland, the "Non-Black Earth Zone," many farms function more as welfare and old-age support agencies than as economic enterprises. But private farmers and small cooperatives do not yet produce very much, although there are now some individual success stories in the RSFSR. So changing the environment for the large farms is the only available way to quickly increase domestically-produced food supplies.

As agricultural reforms began in the late 1980s, Soviet theorists found the solution to these problems of defending the farms from monopoly suppliers and purchasers in the creation of a network of new-style agricultural cooperatives which would share only the name with the old statist "consumers' cooperatives" which had long existed to serve the countryside. Aleksandr Nikonov, president of the All-Union Lenin Agricultural Academy (VASKhNIL) and a long-time advisor to USSR President Mikhail Gorbachev, outlined one of the most thorough versions of a reorganization of Soviet agriculture based on cooperatives.[11] His model, most succinctly articulated at the Fourth Congress of Kolkhozniki in March 1988, advocated a hierarchy of cooperatives all the way from primary producers to the national level. He proposed:

As the first level of cooperation, the primary labor collective is the foundation. Next is the kolkhoz or sovkhoz as a cooperative of contracting independent labor collectives. Next is the agrofirm, the association, and the combine, and finally is the cooperative union. In this way, the entire agroindustrial complex is built on the principles of vertical and horizontal cooperation.[12]

Cooperatives Give Farmers Leverage

The voluntary formation of the new cooperative order was central to Nikonov's vision of rural restructuring. Instead of peasants receiving orders from above, their cooperatives would provide them with leverage to negotiate with suppliers and purchasers. Gorbachev's own speech at the Congress of Kolkhozniki was an expansive, but less specific, statement of similar ideas on the importance of agricultural management through a hierarchy of voluntary cooperatives rather than the existing command-administrative methods.[13]

Within the kolkhozy or sovkhozy, the farm brigades are converted into independent cooperatives operating on full *khozraschet.*[14] In principle, they possess complete control over their own assets once they are leased from the farm, as well as an independent bank account and legal identity. In turn, the farm management's role shifts from commanding the peasants to coordinating their activities. Making the kolkhoz or sovkhoz a "cooperative of cooperatives" greatly reduces the management tasks and the administrative personnel needed. The idea of allowing contractual relations rather than command to regulate relations among the farm's various production cooperatives, leaving only a small "management link" to run things on the farm and negotiate with outsiders, goes back to the 1960s experimenter, Ivan Khudenko, whose trial farm was eventually shut down on Brezhnev's orders. Convicted on a trumped-up charge of embezzling state funds, Khudenko died in jail.[15] This history makes such changes particularly unpalatable to older members of the agricultural administrative bureaucracy and to survivors of the Brezhnev-era party elite.

The relatively few farms which have attempted to reorganize and reduce their staffs by becoming "cooperatives of cooperatives" along these lines since the mid-1980s have found the transition exceedingly difficult because of pressure from above to continue reporting, fulfilling, and delivering in the old way.[16] The best-known models of such cooperatives are peasant farms in the Pytalovskii rayon in Pskov oblast.[17] (There, however, no farms have been completely "cooperativized.") This experiment enjoys VASKhNIL President Nikonov's direct patronage. Since December 1990, many more farms have begun to reform themselves. Adoption of RSFSR laws on land reform and the peasant economy in late 1990 spurred the process of reorganization as some farms have broken up, and some others have reorganized themselves into joint-stock operations or "associations of peasant farms" in order to defend themselves against dissolution. But most farms still seem to operate in the old way.

In order to improve food processing and cut the enormous waste of produce grown that can neither be moved nor stored on site, a party resolution of September 1987 eliminated the prohibition on sideline industries and called for the creation of small processing and producing cooperatives to carry out these tasks on the farms themselves.[18] A logical accompaniment to this measure was the reorganization of off-farm supply, procurement and retail sales agencies as farm cooperatives, or their direct incorporation into the farms.

The March 1989 CPSU plenum approved three basic organizational models to replace the RAPOs for managing agriculture and integrating suppliers and procurement agencies at the district level. Those models were:

• The agroindustrial association (APO), uniting a district's farms "horizontally" with the rayon's other agricultural enterprises;

• The agrofirm (agrofirma), joining a single farm "vertically" with transportation, processing, and retail units; and

• The agrocombine (agrokombinat), integrating a district's farms and other agricultural enterprises "horizontally," as well as creating a "vertical" combination of suppliers, farmers, processors, and retailers.

The earliest of these models to appear in practice was the agrocombine. Unlike its predecessor, the RAPO, which joined the farms with just supply, construction, and food processing agencies in a given district, the agrocombine also included the procurement agencies and could go outside of the district to open its own brand-name retail stores in urban areas. The component parts of the agrocombine apparently lose their status as legally-independent enterprises. The first agrocombine, the APK "Kuban," in the Timashevskii rayon of Krasnodar kray, was established as an experiment in 1984. It transferred all the district specialists to consulting cooperatives that work on contract for the farms and demolished most of the district and farm-level management apparatus. Its director, Mikhail Lomach, claims that if all farms were to begin to process their output on site, as he does, assortments and sales of many foods could be doubled or tripled within three years.[19] By early 1987, Gosagroprom First Deputy Chairman Aleksandr Ievlev reported 22 agrocombines had been formed: 13 in the Russian republic, four in the Ukraine, two each in Kazakhstan and Byelorussia and one in Uzbekistan.[20] By January 1, 1990, there were 204 agrocombines in the USSR, 130 of them in the Russian republic.[21]

An agrofirm specializes in one or a few products, combining one or more farms with processing plants, transportation, and retail sales outlets in a single enterprise. The "Adazhi" kolkhoz in Latvia is the best-known model agrofirm. This agrofirm was created on the basis of an extremely successful kolkhoz in 1986.[22] By January 1, 1990, 198 agrofirms were operating throughout the USSR, including 53 in the RSFSR.[23]

The "agroindustrial association" (APO) is a variant of the agrocombine. Like the agrocombine, the APO includes all the farms, supply and procurement agencies in a given rural district (rayon). Unlike the agrocombine, it is a joint-stock association whose shareholders are the constituent farms and organizations, governed by a council of their representatives.[24] The model for this kind of organization was set up in the Novomoskovskiy rayon of Tula oblast in early 1987.[25] This district was chosen for the experiment because it is the site of Vasily Starodubtsev's model Lenin Collective Farm, and Starodubtsev became the chairman of the new APO.[26] On January 1, 1990, 222 APOs existed in the entire Soviet Union, including 150 in Russia.[27]

Nikonov's 1988 nation-wide cooperative union proposal has been realized in the RSFSR Agrarian Union and the USSR Peasants' Union. It is unlikely that the VASKhNIL president would acknowledge intellectual paternity of these organizations, however.[28] These unions demanded control over the agricultural administrative and supply agencies, as well as quasi-governmental powers as the sole representatives of the peasantry, including a seat for their chairman on the CPSU Politburo. They have become almost exclusively organizations of conservative farm chairmen and directors.[29] Starodubtsev, the elected head of both the Russian and USSR Unions, was a member of the short-lived August 1991 junta.

None of these new organizations improved or fundamentally changed the organization of command agriculture. *Pravda* editorially complained that "the agrocombines, agrofirms, and associations inherited all the worst features of the RAPO," and "economic methods of management are being mastered extremely slowly."[30] All these devices suffer from a similar defect, (which looked like an advantage to the farm chairmen and local officials struggling to hold onto their power), their monopoly position. The district RAPOs, agrocombines, and APOs have monopolized supplies, processing, and sales for their constituents, whether kolkhozy, sovkhozy, or independent farmers. The national peasant unions had the same intent, though they were less successful in realizing their monopoly dreams.

Since the agrocombines and APOs have been created largely in areas where farms were doing well anyway, they make seemingly attractive partners for foreign joint ventures. Both the "Kuban" agrocombine and the Adazhi agrofirm (now reorganized as a joint-stock combine) have concluded deals with foreign food processors, for instance. But because these units are built on the old kolkhozy and sovkhozy and the old agricultural administration's monopoly control of the farms' environment, the APOs and agrocombines are unlikely to make good long-term business partners for foreigners. As their environment changes, so will the associations and combines, and many will probably disappear as the political institutions that supported them continue to wither away.

The Emerging New Structures

The Stalinist system relied on its web of party and state bureaucracies to link the farms to politics and the market. With the end of party discipline, individual farms have no incentive to produce foodstuffs at a loss on command for distant cities. As a result, food supplies in the nation's two capitals, Moscow and Leningrad, have been greatly reduced in the past two years. Rational farm managers sell their produce close to home, barter it for needed inputs, or hold it off the market in anticipation of future higher prices. Since the USSR authorities announced in August 1990 that purchase prices would go up as of January 1, 1991, it is hardly surprising that food shipments to the cities declined during the last quarter of 1990. Similar processes help to explain the repeated food shortages in the winter of 1991. Not only was the overall harvest much smaller than the bumper crop of 1990, but the incentives to retain produce on the farm or in the immediate producing region increased both because of rapid prices increases and the breakup of the old unified Soviet market.

Before new, economic and political institutions could, or can, develop, the old system had to be pried open. A major organizational force for change in the Russian countryside has been the Association of Peasant Farms and Agricultural Cooperatives of Russia (AKKOR), a voluntary interest group established with the help of considerable central pressure. Unlike the organizations sketched earlier, AKKOR does not aim to set up a monopoly. Instead, it considers its job to be the establishment of alternate sources of supply and sales, as the recent establishment of a materials and commodity exchange by the Moscow oblast's AKKOR illustrates. Nor does AKKOR claim to represent all rural interests, limiting its declared constituency to individual farmers and small production cooperatives.

But AKKOR has now been built into the structure of the RSFSR State Committee on Land Reform and the Support of Peasant Farms. Its president, Vladimir Bashmachnikov, is simultaneously a deputy chairman of the committee. Local AKKOR groups pass on the fitness of applicants to receive land for individual farms. AKKOR has charge of distributing the billion rubles allocated by the Russian government to support the creation of peasant farms when the land reform legislation was adopted in 1990. The state support needed to establish AKKOR and its privileged position in the RSFSR government mean that AKKOR could become a new monopolist.[31] The association has already been split by a debate about its relation to the government. (Its executive committee narrowly voted to allow Bashmachnikov to join his government and association posts.)

Unless a variety of similar groups rapidly develop to compete with AKKOR, it, and the Russian republic land reform, may become little more than instruments for the same kind of high-pressure reorganization as collectivization was 60 years ago. For farmers caught in the transition to marke,t there can be little distinction between their suppliers and buyers, and their political interests. They must get out from under the state monopolies which have controlled all aspects of their lives. But if a new state-supported monopoly comes to speak for all of agriculture in place of the old one, little will have changed.

Now that the old structures have collapsed, however, there are hopeful signs that new, local, competitive structures will develop to link farms and the large urban markets. Commodity exchanges have begun to replace the party district secretary as the mechanism for exchanging scarce resources among farms. The biggest exchange, the All-Union Agroindustrial Complex Commodities Exchange, founded in July 1990, still operates largely on a face-to-face basis, with people offering items to exchange making their own individual deals.[32] Middleman cooperatives, such as the Moscow

"Ekonom," the first to assemble a complete mailing list of all Soviet farms from which they can do targeted advertising, specialize in putting together deals for farms with produce to sell to other farms or abroad.[33] Similarly, a mid-1991 article estimated that 150 to 200 cooperatives in each oblast of central Russia are now engaged in trade. Granted, their turnover is still small, perhaps not a thousandth part of the state trade networks, but such cooperatives' very existence is a heartening sign.[34]

Much of this trade is now barter. The return to a barter economy is hardly surprising since much of the unofficial trade between enterprises, which made the old economy operate, always was barter, and the ruble is on the point of being completely devalued. But as the state trade and processing network withers away because more and more goods, in particular more and more foodstuffs, are being sold at much higher "commercial" (free-market) prices, the need for a stable currency, legal regulation, and reliable communications will become more pressing. In short, merchants, middlemen, and farmers will find that they once again need the mechanisms of a larger economic space which only an effective government can provide. Having separated economics from politics, they will find that their new economic interests draw them back into politics, but as citizens, not state functionaries. At that point they will be driven to begin the slow process of recreating a government which can govern to replace the current decree mills which do little but worsen the paper shortage.

The decay and dissolution of the old Soviet system is probably not yet done. But it is now far enough advanced that the cells of a new economy, and a new polity, are beginning to form. The old regime could not be reformed, as its collapse when Gorbachev tried to reconstruct it demonstrated. Rather than worrying about how to strengthen it by suggesting better laws or agreeing to give it additional billions in stabilization funds, concerned observers, business people, and policy makers in the West should attempt to work with the individuals and small groups who are creating a new system out of the chaos of the old. Such assistance will not be as splashy as big programs or "grand bargains," but it is more likely to help achieve the ultimate end of a group of stable, democratic successor states in place of the Soviet empire, and a countryside prosperous, pleasant, and able to feed the Russian population.

Footnotes

1. There has been little practical difference between collective farms (*kolkhoz*, plural *kolkhozy)* and state farms (*sovkhoz*, plural *sovkhozy*) since the mid-1960s when kolkhozy were ordered to begin paying state-guaranteed wages to all their members.

2. See Cynthia S. Kaplan, *The Party and Agricultural Crisis Management in the USSR* (Cornell: Cornell University Press, 1987) for a description of farm management during the late Stalinist era.

3. I have described reforms within the kolkhozy and sovkhozy in "The Return of Individual Farming in the Soviet Union," Geonomics Occasional Paper, No. 1 (October 1991).

4. From lowest to highest, the hierarchy of territorial units was: farm brigade, kolkhoz or sovkhoz, district (*rayon*), province (*oblast*), territory (*kray*), republic, and USSR. The kray division is used only when the smaller province it contains is ethnically defined. So Gorbachev's home region, Stavropol, is a kray because it includes the Karachaevo-Cherkess autonomous oblast, a "homeland" for that small nationality.

5. A "nomenklatura" is literally a list of jobs. A "nomenklatura" position could be filled only if the person selected for the post were approved by the CPSU committee responsible for that post. People whose jobs required such approval formed the self-perpetuating elite of Soviet society, so that "the nomenklatura" has become synony-mous with the old ruling class.

6. I. Lukinov, "Zatraty i tseny v sel'skom khozyaystve: pochemu oni rastut?" *Kommunist,* no. 3 (February 1989), pp. 26-27.

7. The drive by the best to get off the farms explains why the Soviet consistently train many times the number of agricultural machine operators needed yet seemingly never have enough. Once a young man knows how to drive a tractor, he can always get a city job, although usually only with a limited residence permit.

8. Paul Quinn-Judge, "Sogra Postcard: Absolut Hell," *The New Republic* (December 31, 1990), pp. 12-13.

9. William Liefert, "Growing Soviet Food Shortages: A Result of Economy-Wide Monetary Imbalance," Geonomics Occasional Paper, No. 2 (October 1991).

10. N. Kozlov, "Ne vyzhidat', a deystvovat': Dolzhny rukovoditeli, formiruyushchie novye organy upravleniya APK," *Ekonomicheskaya gazeta,* no. 39 (September 1989), pp. 14-15.

11. On Nikonov's influence, see Don Van Atta, "Theorists of Agrarian Perestroika," *Soviet Economy,* vol. 5, no. 1 (January-March 1989), pp. 70-99.

12. A.A. Nikonov, speech at IV Congress of Kolkhozniki, March 25, 1988, in *Chetvertyi vsesoiuznyi s"ezd kolkhoznikov: stenograficheskiy otchet* (Moscow: VO "Agropromizdat," 1988), pp. 201-204 at p. 203.

13. *Sel'skaia zhizn'* (March 24, 1988), pp. 2-4.

14. *Khozraschet,* or "economic accounting," means profit-and-loss accounting. That keeping track of production costs and income should be considered a major reform suggests the scale of the problem of rebuilding agriculture in the former USSR.

15. Alexander Yanov, *The Drama of the Soviet 1960s: A Lost Reform* (Berkeley: Institute of International Studies, University of California, n.d. [1984]); Don Van Atta, "The 'Ivan Khudenko' Sovkhoz–A Guarantee that the Lease Contract will be Permanent?" *Radio Liberty Research*, 511/88 (October 23, 1988).

16. Vladimir Fomin, "Po vsem krest'yanskim pravilam," *Don*, no. 7 (July 1988), pp. 127-133 at p. 129.

17. V. Vorob'ev and V. Somov, "Pytalovskiy proryv: Arenda vozvrashchaet lyudey sela k polnokrovnoy zhizni, vedet k prodovol'stvennomu dostatku," *Pravda* (September 5, 1988), p. 2.

18. "V Tsentral'nom Komitete KPSS: Tsentral'nyy Komitet KPSS prinial postanovlenie 'O neotlozhnykh merakh po uskoreniyu resheniya prodovol'stvennogo vorposa' v sootvetstviy s ustanovkami iyun'skogo (1987 g.) Plenuma TsK KPSS," *Pravda* (September 25, 1987), p. 1.

19. K. Aksenov, "Pered plenumom tsk kpss: Chem 'lechit'' defitsit," *Pravda* (March 4, 1989), p. 2.

20. A. Uglanov, "The USSR State Agro-Industrial Committee's First Year," *Argumenty i fakty* (April 25-May 1, 1987, pp. 1-2), as translated in *Current Digest of the Soviet Press*, vol. 39, no. 19, pp. 20-21 at 21. Gosagroprom, the USSR State Agro-Industrial Committee, was a "superministry" uniting the Ministry of Agriculture and a group of input agencies. Formed in 1985, it was disbanded in 1989.

21. A.V. Gorbunov and V.I. Nilipovskiy, "Organizatsiya upravleniya agro-promyshlennymi kombinatami," *Ekonomika sel'skokhoziaistvennykh i pererabatyvayushchikh predpriyatiy*, no. 2 (February 1991), p. 13.

22. A.E. Kauls, *Rasskazyvayut peredoviki proizvodstva: poisk novogo* (Moscow: 1987).

23. Gorbunov and Nilipovskiy, op. cit.

24. A. Artem'ev, "Na kooperativnoi osnove," *Partiynaya zhizn'*, no. 12 (June 1989), pp. 15-19.

25. "Po puti integratsii," *Pravda*, (April 11, 1987), p. 3.

26. For Starodubtsev's official biography, see "Sostav Tsentral'nogo Komiteta KPSS, izbrannogo XXVIII S"ezdom KPSS," *Izvestiya TsK KPSS*, no. 12 (December 1990).

27. Gorbunov and Nilipovskiy, op. cit.

28. When Nikonov described the kind of agricultural management system he wanted to install in an interview a few months after the Congress of Kolkhozniki, this national level of cooperatives was simply omitted, suggesting he had reconsidered the idea of one, national farm organization. A.A. Nikonov and A.E. Kauls, "Delegaty XIX vsesoyuznoy partkonferentsii na stranitsakh 'Kommunista': Problema nomer odin," *Kommunist*, no. 11 (July 1988), pp. 3-10 at p. 5.

29. See Don Van Atta, "Political Mobilization in the Russian Countryside: Creating Social Movements From Above," pp. 43-73 in Judith B. Sedaitis and Jim Butterfield, eds., *Perestroika from Below: Social Movements in the Soviet Union* (Boulder, Colorado: Westview, 1991).

30. "Partiya i krest'yanstvo," *Pravda* (September 5, 1989), p. 1.

31. On the history of AKKOR and its "central" origins, see Van Atta, "Political Mobilization in the Russian Countryside," op. cit.

32. A. Evstropov and A. Terekhin, "Tovarnye birzhi i rynok kontraktov," *APK: Ekonomika, upravlenie,* no. 8 (August 1991), pp. 73-76 at 73.

33. Personal conversation.

34. Iurii Evstifeev, "Novoe litso v ekonomike: Prodaet tovar 'kupets'?" *Sel'skaya nov'*, no. 7 (July 1991), pp. 16-19 at 16.

Improving the Performance of the Agricultural Trading System

Leader: Juliet Zavon
Director, Soviet Joint Venture Analysis
Archer Daniels Midland Company

Assistant: Heidi Spear, Middlebury College

The agricultural trading system moves crops and livestock from the farm through processing and retail sales to the consumer. These activities cover a significant share of a nation's gross national product, and involve such disparate segments of an economy as wholesale trade, banking, transport, storage, packaging, imports, and exports. Recommendations for improvement in any one of these areas in the Soviet Union (USSR, Soviet Union, or Soviet refer in this paper to the nations occupying the territory of the former USSR.) would be a worthy topic.

The group based its recommendations on the following objectives:
• To encourage a more stable and peaceful USSR;
• To strengthen the USSR as a trading partner;
• To help the Soviet people through a transition period that has great uncertainties and potential privations.

Rather than focus its recommendations on macroeconomic policies that depend on political decisions in the Soviet Union, the group strove to formulate specific recommendations that could be made to the U.S. government, industry associations, foundations, or citizens' groups.

The group recognized that many of the economic structures in the USSR must change in order to improve the agricultural trading system, such as freeing prices and stabilizing the money supply. For instance, if commerce is based on money instead of barter, the distribution system will improve. The macroeconomic changes necessary are already well documented. Therefore, the group focused on other issues and made the following recommendations.

1. Feeding People and Animals for the Next Eight Months
The winter of 1991-1992 is critical, and the critical period will continue through the harvest of the winter grain crop in the early summer of 1992. There is neither potential famine nor an overall food shortage in the USSR. However, it is increasingly difficult to get food in the big cities and feed on the farms, (Farms refer to state, collective, and private farms.) largely because the old state-run distribution system is disintegrating without a replacement.

• **Food Assistance to Develop a Market Economy**
U.S. donated food (as distinguished from grain) should be sold for rubles in critical food-deficit regions (Moscow, Leningrad, Kiev, Sverdlovsk, and others to be chosen by size of population or strategic importance) through the emerging commodity exchanges and private wholesale and retail networks. Food distribution should help, not hurt, the emerging market system and should not support the old state-controlled system.

• **Financial Assistance for People with Low Incomes**
Rubles received from sale of food through market channels should be used to establish a fund to supplement the income of the neediest segments of the population so they can purchase the U.S.-supplied food. As a secondary objective, this fund can be used to support people-to-people contacts described in recommendation 3.

• **Feed Assistance to Develop a Market Economy**
Livestock are being slaughtered because of a feed shortage. This distress slaughtering will reduce the USSR's ability to produce animal products and will reduce the potential market for U.S. feed grains for the next three to five years, because livestock cycles in the USSR are longer than in the West. The United States should supply feed through the emerging market channels described above and use revenues similarly. While we have livestock data by republic, we know little about the emerging commercial channels between port, farm, processor, and city.

To preserve livestock and help feed the cities, program administrators must quickly identify transportation links and the production that is optimally located to serve food-deficit cities.

2. The GATT Negotiations and the USSR
The United States should strive toward and urge conciliation to successfully conclude the current negotiations under the General Agreement on Tariffs & Trade (GATT). It would provide the nations of the world, including the USSR, greater access to markets and a more realistic trading environment. Equally important, it would provide the USSR with examples of appropriate agricultural policies.

The following example is offered as an illustration, not a specific recommendation, of what is meant by appropriate agricultural policies. Many nations set prices for agricultural commodities to insure that farmers have adequate income. This destroys the price-setting formula of the market and skews market signals that influence production decisions. Taxpayers pay for this policy through government subsidies or the cost of storing surplus commodities. This could be avoided by letting the market set prices and by setting up an insurance program to supplement farm incomes in years when farm revenues are low, either because of crop failures or low market prices. In addition, consumers would benefit from lower-cost food.

3. Preparing for a Market Economy
The working group acknowledged that substantial improvement in the agricultural trading system will be quite limited until the necessary macroeconomic changes are made, such as stabilizing the money supply, and until a new legal working relationship is functioning between the republics of the former USSR. Given this situation, the group recommends expanding people-to people contacts at all levels in both the Soviet Union and United States. The exchange of ideas and exposure, whether in banking, worker safety, or literature will facilitate communication and encourage new ways of resolving problems.

 • **Improving Management and Plant Operations**
The way to change management is not by training a new management elite schooled in Western business practices in a classroom far from the work place but by on-the-job training. The next-best option is internships or study tours designed for mid-career professions, a category which should include not only the managers of a plant, but also the plant's engineers, mechanics, accountants, and economic planners.

There are industry associations in the United States for every component of the agricultural trading system, whether the subject is packaging equipment or feed milling. These associations and their members companies could be instrumental in designing and implementing practical exchange programs.

 • **Exchanges and Contacts at All Levels**
School or university exchange programs, sister-city programs, farm-to-farm exchange programs, and other programs of this sort should be encouraged and supported.

 • **Simplify and Facilitate the Visa Process**
Remove the existing restrictions on the number of visas the United States will grant the Soviet Union for farmer exchange programs.

Agribusiness Stategies

Leader: Jim Stafford, Director, International Services
Division, Holstein Association
Co-Leader: Steve Kerr, Chief Executive Officer
   Holstein Association

Assistants: Elisha S. Hall, Middlebury College
   Stacey Fallon, Middlebury College

Purpose: Evaluate the condition of agriculture in the Soviet Union
and Baltic republics and develop specific strategies to enable U.S.
firms to enter these markets. Establish guidelines and criteria for
interaction among Soviet and American agribusinesses. The group
approached the topics from two different perspectives. First, the group
identified specific steps or strategies that individual firms could implement
to take advantage of business opportunities in the former Soviet Union.
Second, the group examined how U.S. agribusinesses in conjunction with
the U.S. government could help create a macroeconomic climate and
market infrastructure in the Soviet Union that would be more conducive to
Western trade and investment.

Strategies for Doing Business in the Soviet Union

Before attempting to enter the Soviet market, Western agribusinesses
should analyze their own capabilities, gather pertinent market information,
and develop their own strategies. The following points should be considered:

• Businesses must assess their own ability to assume and manage risk and
decide how long they can wait to have a positive cash flow and to be
profitable in hard currency.

• Businesses must decide if they need consultants to determine the most
advantageous political, geographic, and infrastructural location for trade
and investment. Businesses should pay particular attention to political
institutions and newly developing private farmers' organizations, such as
AKKOR, which may help or hinder trade and investment.

• Firms should start at the "grassroots" level and work up the bureaucratic ladder. Higher-level bureaucrats should be involved only when they have the potential to block projects at later stages of the project. As agriculture is decentralized, grassroots relationships will become increasingly important.

• Well capitalized firms with aggressive risk management strategies may be content to receive little or no hard currency from business ventures for several years. These "beach head operations," could vary from an office with a telephone to a McDonald's franchise. The likelihood of obtaining significant hard currency returns in the short term is minute; therefore, such businesses would be faced with accepting rubles and/or countertrade. Specialized companies can facilitate such transactions. Barter may be an unavoidable first step and shorten the time before hard currency returns are possible. Barter, on the other hand, adds another layer of complexity to making a successful venture, especially for small and medium- sized businesses.

• Businesses must not only be concerned with selling their own products in the Soviet Union but also with obtaining saleable products to redeem for hard currency from third parties. In any case, the Soviet market can probably not be approached with short-term profit objectives. Current economic and legal realities in the Soviet Union dictate that most businesses should consider risking only those resources which they can afford to lose. For example, the current war of laws can cause investments to be lost with a stroke of the pen.

• Effective business strategies cannot be developed from a distance or in a vacuum. Any firm seriously contemplating trade, investment, or joint ventures must personally assess the situation on site. Consulting firms can do much of the basic market research and search for prospective partners, but this does not remove the necessity for the organization's personal involvement. It is most important for Western firms to provide continuity in personnel assigned to project development.

• One of the major business constraints, particularly for small firms with limited resources, is the lack of information on the availability of raw materials and labor and on changing legal regulations. The working group suggested both private and public solutions. First, private organizations, either Soviet or American, could assemble information and disseminate it to potential investors. Second, the U.S. government should increase the number and distribution of commercial officers in the consulates and embassy and mandate that they gather and disseminate commercially strategic information.

Investment Criteria

Group members doing business in the Soviet Union suggested the following criteria:

- Projects should be in a company's core business line.
- Ventures must be technically and financially sound.
- U.S. firms should have managerial control regardless of the size of their equity.
- Projects should be self-sufficient in hard currency, either through direct sale of products or through barter.
- In the absence of a free-market structure and trade protection treaties, some firms may require profitability guarantees, in addition to protection from confiscation, from the United States or Soviet governments.
- Projects must have strong support from local institutions and reform groups.
- Tacit approval by the republican government in addition to local government is desirable to decrease the chance of last-minute obstacles.
- The geographical region should have an ongoing indigenous privatization program.

There are also numerous constraints in the Soviet Union well beyond the scope and control of individual firms. To create a more favorable environment, the working group suggested the following steps: unrestricted internal and external free trade, unregulated pricing, increased interrepublic trade, removal of export controls, implementation of a market-based economy and legal system, government programs to stimulate entrepreneurship, government safety nets for the those displaced by reforms, and training programs for business managers.

Western governments can assist in this process by:

- Providing financing guarantees, through the Foreign Credit Insurance Association (FCIA).
- Providing humanitarian aid that does not discourage or disrupt local distribution systems.
- Removing subsidies and liberalizing their own foreign trade.

Business-Government Cooperation Is Needed

U.S. businesses will not invest significantly in the present Soviet Union while the old system is falling apart, and there is no new infrastructure. The group examined a variety of strategies for business and government to work cooperatively to help build a macroeconomic infrastructure in the Soviet Union conducive to supporting a market economy and Western investment.

There was strong support for the following initiatives and concepts:

• U.S. government resources should be redirected from short-term fixes, such as shipping subsidized commodities, to long-term solutions, such as assisting the development of commodity exchanges and free-market mechanisms; from financial assistance to assisting in the establishment of financial institutions.

• Soviet agricultural problems stem from poor productivity/efficiency and distribution, not from the overall quantity of production. Convincing statistical evidence indicates that the shortages of food in urban areas result primarily from the inability and/or unwillingness of the producers to market the production through the state distribution channels. Soviet grain harvests, for example, have ranged from 160 to 240 million tons during the past decade while total human and animal consumption requires about 140 to 150 million tons. However, as much as 20 percent of the harvest is lost in harvesting, storage, processing, and distribution. Collective farms have met less than half their state orders this year, which has compounded the shortages created by a poor harvest.

However, the media has probably overplayed the "disaster" concept. This should be brought to the attention of public policy makers. That is not to minimize regional shortages, distribution bottlenecks, or the resulting real hardships. It may well be desirable and necessary for Western governments to provide various forms of humanitarian aid, but this effort should not become the basis of the long-term economic or trade relationship between the West and the former Soviet Union.

• If humanitarian food aid is to be provided, this aid should be distributed through the newly created commodity exchanges rather than simply placed into state food outlets.

• The United States should develop an international economic trade and development policy that complements the private sector's interests in the Soviet Union and the Baltic republics. The government's ability to promote international business development is seriously constrained by turf battles, incessant red tape, and lack of continuity in trade policy.

• The private sector alone does not have the resources to oversee infrastructural development in the Soviet Union, however, the private sector can and should provide technical expertise and management help for government initiatives.

• The government has no coordinated plan to help the Soviet Union develop a market economy. U.S. government and industry should cooperate to promote private investment through a private-sector advisory council or a joint government-private sector board financed by the U.S. government. This body would be responsible for jointly identifying, prioritizing, and implementing infrastructural development and training projects.

• U.S. and Soviet participants agreed that lack of knowledge and understanding of market systems within the Soviet business and government community is a major constraint to Western trade and investment. Business people representing retail, wholesale, manufacturing, and farm operations need to be sent for extended periods of time to the Soviet Union to provide training at all levels. "Put good people over there, and U.S. business will find a way to take advantage of them," said one participant.

• Another constraint is the absence of a legal framework. The business advisory council could establish teams of lawyers to work with their Soviet counterparts to help create basic business law. If such efforts were coordinated through a single entity, this could result in a more comprehensive legal structure and one in which Western business could have a significant input. An Agency for International Development program, for example, supports American law and accounting firms working with Eastern European ministries.

• The U.S. government could also cooperate with the private sector by expanding the role of the Overseas Private Investment Corporation (OPIC). OPIC was established primarily to facilitate private sector overseas investment in the Third World by providing FCIA insurance and operating capital for these investments. The agency's role should be expanded to provide comprehensive assistance to U.S. firms investing in the Soviet Union and Baltic republics.

• The IMF has completed a useful study that provides potential investors with general suggestions and background information on investing in the Soviet Union. This information is necessary but is not sufficient to provide the basis for investment decisions. Aside from official initiatives and programs, there will continue to be smaller efforts, with or without government backing, to address specific needs such as the People to People program.

In summary, Western firms seeking to do business in the Soviet Union need to analyze their risk management and time constraints thoroughly before making investment decisions. Companies are advised to do personal research on site, to get down in the trenches and observe what is going on, and to decide who may or may not be a suitable business partner.

Business development with the West will, however, continue at a slow pace until the central and republican governments disengage themselves from production and distribution decisions and until market-oriented legal and financial structures emerge. These activities are currently under way but without any coordination. There is an immediate need for a sustained effort on the part of U.S. business interests and government institutions to participate in this process. The goal would be to provide a coordinated approach toward the establishment of free-market laws, financial structures, and marketing institutions. The real challenge is coordinating this assistance to ensure the timely development of a comprehensive system.

Finance and Investment Stategies

Leader: Keith Severin, Senior Associate for Soviet Affairs
  E. A. Jaenke and Associates, Inc.

Assistant: Catherine Lee, Middlebury College

I nvesting in the Soviet Union has always required patience and realistic expectations. This is even more true since the failed coup in
mid-August. More unrest is possible if conditions in the food and
agricultural sector do not quickly improve.

The great uncertainty about the country's political and economic
stability has increased the apprehensiveness of foreign investors at a time
when the need for outside investment is greater than ever. Political calculations will weigh heavily in decisions of Western governments, businesses,
and other important interests to assist the Soviet Union, for much is at stake.

This report doesn't include the recommendations of Secretary of
Agriculture Madigan from his recent trip to the Soviet Union, as he has not
yet reported to President Bush.

Nonetheless, working group participants agreed that outside investment in the Soviet food and agricultural sphere will be limited — a few
billion dollars from all sources. Several factors will limit investment: 1.
Investor apprehension stemming from the unsettled political situation in
the Soviet Union; 2. The slow pace and uncertain direction of Soviet
reforms; 3. Tight budgets and the general state of Western economies.

Funds must be limited to priority projects. Judicious use of outside
resources will also help ensure that domestic funds will be used more
responsibly. Soviets will be encouraged to show that they are using their own
resources efficiently in order to encourage additional Western assistance.
At the same time, outside funding should be channelled through new free-
market institutions and networks, to the extent possible, to strengthen them
and give them credibility. Since financial assistance will be limited, projects
should be coordinated through international bodies, such as the G-7, IMF,
and the World Bank.

Investment Priorities

The group first identified projects to improve the food and agricultural sector that will require new or additional financing. Those projects are listed below, along with recommendations on the most appropriate sources for funding. Clearly, some projects require long-term capital investment, such as those dealing with infrastructure. Others, such as annual crop and livestock production projects, require shorter-term investment.

The highest priorities in reforming Soviet agriculture are:

• Storage at all levels. Losses can range from 25 to 30 percent of grains to 50 percent and more of perishables, such as vegetables, fruits, and livestock products.

• Creation of food distribution chains in selected major cities. Refrigerated transport and storage are essential, for example, for perishables. Warehousing is inadequate, both quantitatively and qualitatively. Additional food outlets and stores are needed in bigger cities to reduce lines.

• Construction of road networks connecting farms to hard surfaces. Rural farmers must use horses to reach surfaced roads during spring thaws when country roads are seas of mud.

Crucial to the entire process is the development of rural banks to provide credit to small farmers and financial and commodity exchanges to create competitive markets for farm produce. A list of critical needs follows:

1. Internal Road Networks: All-weather roads are needed, especially in the non-black soil region. Roadbeds and drainage are also necessary. These projects could be financed locally and constructed with local materials.

2. Social Infrastructure: The state and collective farms' "stranglehold" on the provision of health care, veterinary facilities, schools, and all programs of rural life, must be broken. The entire life of farm workers is centered in the village of the state or collective farm. There are no alternative choices or opportunities. Foreign and domestic funding will be needed to create a new, broader safety net.

3. Production Credit and Long-term Credit for Capital Investment: Individual farmers need to purchase land, equipment, and machinery. Long-term credit is needed for medium- and small-scale processing plant operations and for cooperatives. Short-term production credit can be financed with rubles. Long-term capital investment can be financed with foreign and domestic currency.

4. Expansion of Warehouses: Storage facilities, grain elevators, and frozen food storage, as well as credit for small retail food outlets, is essential to improve the food distribution network and cut waste. A combination of foreign and domestic currency will be required, depending on size and location of operations.

5. Supply-side Financing: The availability of animal feed, fertilizer, spare parts, seeds, chemicals, and packaging materials must be improved. Western hard currency will be needed until this infrastructure is established.

6. Financial and Commodity Exchanges: Security exchanges, computers, and computing machines are needed. Hard currency is needed for equipment and training. These facilities are essential if market mechanisms are to work efficiently and if reforms are to succeed.

7. Rural Bank Structure: A bottom-up process is most effective. Farmers need training in how to manage credit financing. A handful of Soviet students has just begun training in the West. Rural banks must be regional because of the geographic expanse and diversity of agriculture. Hard currency and Western training are needed.

8. Development of Fundamental Agricultural Sciences and Dissemination of Information: Foreign currency is needed for equipment. Modern research laboratory facilities must be built and equipped, including up-to-date computers. A system to disseminate scientific findings to the field, such as the U.S. farm extension service, must be developed.

9. Improved Communications: Foreign equipment and training are necessary in the initial stages. Rural areas badly need telephones and radio systems.

10. Improved Water Supply and Irrigation: There are serious infrastructure problems that must be solved if farms, in general, and farms in water deficit areas, such as Central Asia and southern Ukraine, are to be viable. The bulk of the funding can be domestic currency, with foreign funding for up-to-date irrigation techniques.

Helping the Small Western Investor

Small firms and businesses generally lack the personnel, experience, and financial resources needed to invest in the USSR. They can, however, make decisions more quickly than large corporate firms. Legislation such as the proposed "de la Garza Bill," (H.R. 3556), "Food for Emerging Democracies Act of 1991," could provide this financial, and in some cases, technical and cultural support.

Potential foreign investors should personally visit the Soviet Union to determine Soviet needs and evaluate the feasibility of investment. Personal contact will save time and money for both sides in developing mutually beneficial projects.

Western investors must be aware of the non-agricultural costs of rural investments. Agrarian reform and investment must include all facets of *sel'skaya zhizn* (rural life), not just *sel'skoye khozyaystvo*, (rural economy). The expectation that firms will help fund schools, provide housing and community recreation is a "fact of life" that foreign investors cannot overlook when evaluating business opportunities.

Sell Western Surplus Food to Generate Investment Funds

Selling Western surplus food commodities could be a new and imaginative way to generate investment funds. Such sales would not only use and strengthen existing facilities, but they would also help alleviate current food shortages and would not be a disincentive to Soviet agricultural producers. Food commodities acquired via import under credit, credit guarantees, or humanitarian assistance (donations) would be split and sold through two channels:

1. Private sector, including new commodity exchanges and private retailers, at free-market prices;

2. State stores, accessible only to members of vulnerable segments of the population at controlled prices (a pseudo food-stamp program).

Windfall profits from free-market sales could be taxed to support enterprise funds, grants to poverty groups, and construction of infrastructure. State stores would serve only vulnerable groups. The bulk of the population would be forced to buy through the private/free market. This proposal is one example of how new investment could be introduced into the food and agricultural sector.

Unresolved Questions

Many other factors will influence investment decisions. Who, under the evolving system, will be responsible for repaying the foreign debt — the "Center," republics, farms, enterprises? Will there be free prices? How will profits be taxed? How can profits be repatriated? When will the ruble be convertible?

While time is of the essence, so are patience and understanding. Soviets want to learn Western business principles. Both sides are vastly inexperienced in these new endeavors, but there are ways to find satisfactory solutions. Government-private business advisory groups, that would include representatives of land grant colleges, offer great possibilities and should not be overlooked.

About the Contributors

Keith Bush was director of Radio Liberty Research in Munich from 1975 to 1990 and is now a senior analyst at the new RFE/RL Research Institute. *From the Command Economy to the Market,* a collection of his interviews with prominent Western economists, was published by Dartmouth Publishing Company in 1991.

John J. Cavanaugh is chairman and chief executive officer of Summit Limited, an international trade consulting firm that focuses on the Soviet food industry. Mr. Cavanaugh is a former member of the U.S House of Representatives from Nebraska.

Vera Krylatykh is deputy director of the Agrarian Institute of the All-Union Academy in Moscow. An academician, she has specialized in land reform and agribusiness relations.

Vera Matusevich is professor of agribusiness management at the Academy of National Economy in Moscow. Prof. Matusevich, who has specialized in land reform and the cooperative movement, is a research fellow in residence at the Geonomics Institute during the 1991-92 academic year.

Allan Mustard is deputy coordinator, Eastern Europe and Soviet Secretariat, Foreign Agricultural Service, U.S. Department of Agriculture. A specialist in Soviet agriculture, he was agricultural attache in the U.S. Embassy in Moscow from 1986 to 1988.

Ivar Raig, chairman of the Estonian Rural Center Party, is a member of the Supreme Soviet of Estonia and vice-chairman of the Economic Committee. Dr. Raig, vice-president of the Estonian Society of Economists, has been deeply involved in the planning of that country's transition to a market economy.

Barbara Severin is a senior analyst, specializing in the Soviet economy, at the Central Intelligence Agency.

Gelii Shmelev, head of the agrarian section of the Moscow-based Institute of International Economic and Political Studies, has written widely on private plot agriculture. Among his books are *The Family Takes a Contract* and *Hired Worker or Owner of the Land.*

Vladimir Tikhonov, one of the Soviet Union's most prominent agricultural economist, is president of The Union of Amalgamated Cooperatives, an organization that supports the emerging cooperative movement. Dr. Tikhonov, long a supporter of radical economic reform and the breakup of collective farms, is a member of the Academy of Agricultural Sciences.

Donald Van Atta, assistant professor of government at Hamilton College, has written widely on the organizational structure of Soviet agriculture. He has recently contributed to the following collections: *Political Control of the Soviet Economy* (Cambridge University Press), *Reform and Transformation in Communist Systems: Comparative Perspectives* (Paragon House), and *Perestroika in the Countryside: Agricultural Reform in the Gorbachev Era* (Sharpe).

Karl-Eugen Wädekin, an economist and one of the preeminent scholars of Eastern European and Soviet agriculture, recently retired from the University of Giessen in Bierlingen, Germany. His recent works include *Soviet Agriculture: Reforms and Prospects* and *Communist Agriculture: Farming in the Soviet Union and Eastern Europe.*

About the Editors

Michael P. Claudon is president and managing director of the Geonomics Institute and professor of economics at Middlebury College. He has published numerous articles and books on international economic issues and is a frequent commentator on the reform of the command economies of Eastern Europe and the former Soviet Union. Dr. Claudon is co-editor of four other volumes and serves as series editor for the Geonomics Institute for International Economic Advancement Series. He has a Ph.D from Johns Hopkins University,

Tamar L. Gutner, former research director at the Geonomics Institute, is now a Ph.D. candidate in international relations at the Massachusetts Institute of Technology. She is a former financial reporter for A.P.-Dow Jones and is the author of *The Story of SAIS,* a history of the Johns Hopkins University School of Advanced International Studies.

Seminar Participants

Ilias H. Akhmadov, First private farmer in the Checheno-Ingushskaya ASSR

Kenneth M. Becker, Agricultural Loan Officer,
Vermont Industrial Development Authority (VIDA)

Viktor Ivanovich Bespalov, Vice Chairman
Regional Association of Agricultural Managers, Pereslavl

Tim Bodin, Economic Analysis Department, Commodity Marketing
Division, Cargill, Incorporated

Keith Bush, Senior Analyst, Radio Free Europe/Radio Liberty Research
Institute, Germany

Vikram Capoor, Research Assistant, Geonomics Institute

John Cavanaugh, Chairman and Chief Executive Officer, Summit Limited

Michael P. Claudon, President, Geonomics Institute

Thomas Fogarty, Associate, International Agri-Tech Resources

Robert Foster, President, Foster Farm, Inc.

Thomas M. French, Attorney at Law

Howard S. Gochberg, Vice President, Logistics/Custom Products,
Land O' Lakes, Inc.

Alan Gotlieb, College of Agriculture and Life Sciences, Plant and Soil
Science Department, University of Vermont

George Gramling, Manager, International Technical Cooperation
Programs, Holstein Association

Kenneth Gray, Chief, Centrally Planned Economies Branch, Economic Research Service, United States Department of Agriculture (USDA)

Tamar Gutner, Research Director, Geonomics Institute

Pier Luigi Iacoacci, Economist, Policy Analysis Division, Food and Agriculture Organization of the United Nations (FAO), Rome

Jeremy N. Ingpen, Vice President, Agribusiness, Geonomics Institute

Benjamin S. Jaffray, Chairman, Sheffield Group, Ltd.

Robert A. Jones, Chairman of the Board, Geonomics Institute; Chairman Emeritus, MMS International, Inc.

Steve Kerr, Chief Executive Officer, Holstein Association

Mark Kramer, Writer in Residence, Boston University

Frederick Krimgold, Associate Dean, Virginia Polytechnic Institute and State University

Elmira N. Krylatykh, Academician and Senior Academic Secretary, Division of Agricultural Economics, Organization, and Agrarian Policy, All-Union Academy of Agricultural Sciences (VASKhNIL)

Andres Kurrik, Vice President, AM-RE Managers, Inc.

Allen Liefer, Sales Representative, GMLS Industries, Inc.

David Macey, Chairman, Russian and Soviet Area Studies Program, Middlebury College

Vera Matusevich, Professor of Agribusiness Management, Academy of National Economy, Moscow; Geonomics Research Fellow

Girt Mergins, Manager, USSR and Central Europe, Babson Brothers Company

Stephen Messinger, Assistant Manager, PSR International

Allan Mustard, Deputy Coordinator, Eastern Europe and Soviet Secretariat, Foreign Agricultural Service, USDA

Roger Pajak, National Security Advisor, Office of the Secretary, Department of the Treasury

Ivar Raig, Chairman, Estonian Rural Center Party; Member of the Standing Committee of Foreign Affairs, Supreme Council of the Republic of Estonia

Carl J. Rosenquist, Managing Director, Wyeth Nutritionals, Inc.

Barbara Severin, Senior Analyst, Central Intelligence Agency

Keith Severin, Senior Associate for Soviet Affairs, E. A. Jaenke and Associates, Inc.

Gelii I. Shmelev, Academician and Department Head, Agrarian Institute, VASKhNIL

Jim Stafford, Director, International Services Division, Holstein Association

Vladimir A. Tikhonov, Academician; Member, Congress of People's Deputies; President, Union of Amalgamated Cooperatives

M. Ann Tutwiler, Director, Agribusiness Policy, Central Soya

Don Van Atta, Department of Government, Hamilton College

Karl-Eugen Wädekin, Professor (retired), University of Giessen, Germany

Juliet Zavon, Director, Soviet Joint Venture Analysis, Archer Daniels Midland Company